THE ART OF
LEATHER BRAIDING

THE ART OF LEATHER BRAIDING

BEGINNER'S GUIDE TO MAKING JEWELRY, PENDANTS, BRACELETS, BELTS, STRAPS, AND KEY FOBS

ROY LUO & KELLY TONG

A QUARTO BOOK

Copyright © 2018
Quarto Publishing plc.

First edition for North America published
in 2018 by Barron's Educational Series, Inc.

All inquiries should be addressed to:
Barron's Educational Series, Inc.
250 Wireless Boulevard
Hauppauge, New York 11788
www.barronseduc.com

ISBN: 978-1-4380-1118-9

Library of Congress Control No:
2017951826

QUAR.LRBR

Conceived, designed, and produced by
Quarto Publishing plc
an imprint of The Quarto Group
The Old Brewery
6 Blundell Street
London N7 9BH
www.quartoknows.com

Technical editor: Elise Mann
Editorial assistant: Danielle Watt
Editor: Kate Burkett
Designer: Karin Skanberg
Illustrators: Olya Kamieshkova
and Kuo Kang Chen
Photographers: Simon Pask
and Emma Robinson
Art director: Caroline Guest
Creative director: Moira Clinch
Publisher: Samantha Warrington

Printed in China
9 8 7 6 5 4 3 2 1

CONTENTS

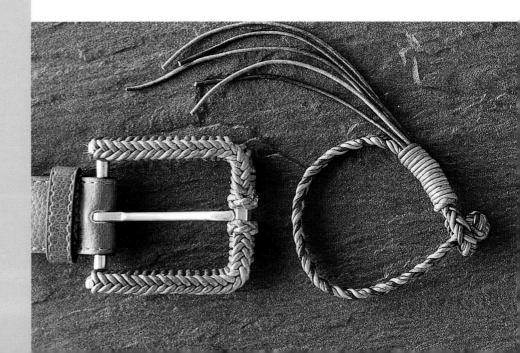

HELLO EVERYONE, IT'S NICE TO MEET YOU. MY NAME IS YINGXIU LUO.

I was born in ChangSha, in HuNan, China. In 2013, I moved to the United States with my wife, Kelly. When I was in China, I worked in the television industry. It was only after moving to the US that I became familiar with leather braiding.

It all began when Kelly gave me a book called *Encyclopedia of Rawhide and Leather Braiding*. To be honest, because my level of English is very limited, I did not learn leather braiding by reading the book, but rather by following the pictures.

After a year, I could complete most of the leather-braiding projects in the book. Once I had perfected those, I started using the basic methods of braiding with different thicknesses and colors of cords to design wearable jewelry and accessories.

My wife and I also love vintage culture, so we began to use leather braiding to repair and recycle items that we found at flea markets.

Leather braiding is a very logical art form. You need to be focused and patient. When I first started, I was very impatient and, whenever I encountered obstacles, I just gave up. After a while, I discovered that I was not looking at the pictures closely enough. For example, the pictures would show braiding from left to right, but I was braiding from right to left.

The key to leather braiding is to understand that there is a process and that every step is important in determining the final outcome of the braid. Without paying meticulous attention to detail, the braid will not be formed correctly—this is often an area of concern for beginners.

However, as you become more familiar with leather braiding and its various techniques, you will find yourself truly enjoying the magic of this craft.

LEATHER BRAIDING IS A VERY LOGICAL ART FORM.

CHAPTER **1**

GETTING STARTED

LEATHER CORDS

YOU CAN USE MANY TYPES OF STRING, INCLUDING THOSE MADE FROM SILK, NYLON, AND SUEDE, FOR BRAIDING. HOWEVER, THE MAIN MATERIAL USED TO CREATE THE JEWELRY IN THIS BOOK IS LEATHER CORD, WHICH CAN BE BRAIDED, KNOTTED, OR WOVEN IN A MULTITUDE OF WAYS, AS WELL AS ATTACHED TO METAL FINDINGS. FOR US, LEATHER MAKES THE BEST MATERIAL FOR BRAIDING BECAUSE, UNLIKE OTHER MATERIALS, IT IS FLEXIBLE, CAN BE WORN CLOSE TO THE SKIN, AND AGES VERY WELL WITH WEAR.

LEATHER AND SUEDE

LEATHER IS THE SKIN OF AN ANIMAL THAT HAS BEEN TANNED AND PRESERVED, AND OFTEN COLORED WITH DYES. IT USUALLY HAS A SMOOTH SIDE, OFTEN WITH A PEBBLY TEXTURE, AND A ROUGHER, TEXTURED SIDE THAT IS REFERRED TO AS SUEDE. SUEDE IS REALLY JUST LEATHER WITH A DISTINCTIVE FURRY TEXTURE. A SUEDE FINISH IS ACTUALLY THE ROUGH INNER SURFACE THAT'S LEFT ONCE THE SMOOTH OUTER LAYER OF THE LEATHER HAS BEEN STRIPPED AWAY. THERE ARE TWO TYPES OF LEATHER CORD: FLAT LACES AND ROUND CORDS.

FLAT LEATHER LACES

Flat laces, which can be made from suede, leather, or rawhide, are measured by their width. The thickness varies, with suede and leather laces being 1-2 mm thick, while rawhide laces are usually much thicker. Suede and leather laces tend to be softer and easier to manipulate. Rawhide lace is tougher and will behave more like round leather cord when you're braiding most projects. The softness of the leather depends on the type of hide used. For example, deerskin leather lace is much softer than regular leather lace, which is usually made from cowhide. Depending on the design, flat laces can be used for braiding, the softer laces for macramé, and the tougher laces as the warp cord in weaving.

ROUND LEATHER CORDS

Round leather cords come in a variety of colors and also in metallic finishes. Leather cords are available in different diameters, ranging from 0.5 mm to 6 mm. This variety of sizes widens the range of effects that can be achieved when braiding, many of which are showcased in this book. Depending on the thickness of the cord and how it has been prepared, some leather cords are softer and more supple than others. We only use round leather cords to braid because, unlike flat cords, the surface of round cords is consistent. This drastically affects the outcome of the finished braids.

FINISHING AND AFTERCARE

1 Store the leather cords in a cool, dry place away from direct sunlight.

2 We prefer to use naturally dyed, heat-sealed leather cord. This type of cord is available in natural colors and preserves the original texture of the leather surface.

3 Leather cords are not easily damaged by water. In fact, we often use water to set the design and shape of pieces of leather jewelry such as rings.

4 Coat items of leather jewelry with leather oil if they are not going to be worn often.

5 Our skin releases natural oil and this oil can be good for leather jewelry. For this reason, the best care for leather items is to wear them frequently.

TOOLS

HAVING THE RIGHT TOOLS AND PIECES OF EQUIPMENT FOR BRAIDING PROJECTS IS JUST AS IMPORTANT AS HAVING THE RIGHT MATERIALS. LUCKILY, LEATHER JEWELRY DOES NOT REQUIRE EXPENSIVE OR HARD-TO-FIND TOOLS.

SCISSORS

Since leather is a tough material, you will need a good pair of sharp scissors. The tip of the scissors needs to be pointed and sharp to help achieve that clean-cut edge. Do not use your braiding scissors to cut other things, such as paper, as this will quickly blunt them.

GLUE

If you are attaching a finished braid to metal findings, you will need to use glue. It's always best to use a brand of glue that has a precise application tip, as this will give you better control.

CHAIN-NOSE PLIERS

These pliers are smooth and flat on the inside, and come to a point at the end. They are useful for helping you thread cords through tight openings and braids.

MEASURING TAPE

A measuring tape is necessary for measuring the cord before you begin to make the jewelry. It is also useful for deciding on the required length of a piece of jewelry before starting a project.

HANDS

Your hands are the most important tool when it comes to leather braiding, as they do most of the work—braiding, knotting, and weaving.

BEGINNING AND FINISHING YOUR BRAID

THERE ARE MANY DIFFERENT WAYS TO START OR FINISH A PROJECT. MOST OF THE PROJECTS IN THIS BOOK BEGIN OR END BY ATTACHING AND GLUING THEM TO METAL FINISHINGS, KNOTTING THEM (SEE *BASIC TECHNIQUES*, PAGES 18–23), OR USING A TECHNIQUE CALLED WHIPPING.

WHIPPING

THIS IS A BASIC WAY OF SECURING LEATHER CORDS. IT CAN BE DONE ANYWHERE ALONG THE LENGTH OF THE SAMPLE, SO YOU CAN CREATE EXACTLY THE LENGTH REQUIRED. USE A STRAND OF THE SAME TYPE OF LEATHER CORD FOUND IN THE PROJECT, SO THAT THE WHIPPING MATCHES THE REST OF THE WORK. HERE A CONTRASTING COLOR HAS BEEN USED TO HIGHLIGHT THE WHIPPING.

ATTACHING FINDINGS

FINDINGS ARE THOSE LITTLE PIECES, USUALLY MADE OF METAL, THAT ENABLE YOU TO FINISH OFF YOUR JEWELRY AND HELP YOU TO CREATE PROFESSIONAL, ATTRACTIVE, AND PRACTICAL PIECES. THERE ARE MANY DIFFERENT VARIETIES, SO IT'S IMPORTANT TO CHOOSE FINDINGS THAT SUIT YOUR JEWELRY.

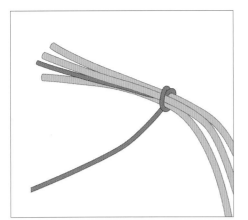

1 Place the whipping cord in the middle of the leather cords you would like to secure. Hold the cords together at the top of the braid; then, depending on where you would like to start the braid, pull the whipping cord out from the center and start coiling it around the other leather cords.

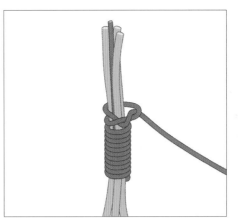

2 Coil the whipping cord until you reach the required length. Knot by wrapping the cord under, then over itself, and pulling tight.

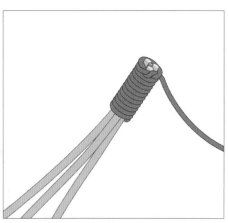

3 Once you have made the knot, cut off any extra whipping cord and the project cords above the knot, and you are ready to begin your braid.

1 Trim off any excess leather cords.

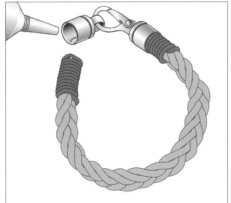

2 Place a drop of glue on the ends of the cords and around the opening of the findings, and insert the cords into the findings. Allow at least two hours for the glue to dry.

BASIC TECHNIQUES

BASIC JEWELRY-MAKING TECHNIQUES ARE THE FOUNDATION OF MAKING LEATHER JEWELRY. EVEN IF YOU HAVE NEVER MADE YOUR OWN JEWELRY BEFORE, YOU WILL QUICKLY BE ABLE TO LEARN THE CORE SKILLS NEEDED.

SQUARE KNOT

A SQUARE KNOT IS A TWO-PART KNOT THAT FORMS A SQUARE SHAPE WHEN PULLED TIGHT.

HALF-HITCH KNOT

THE HALF-HITCH KNOT IS A LOOSE KNOT THAT COILS ONE CORD AROUND ANOTHER, CREATING A HELIX SHAPE. FOR THIS KNOT THERE IS AN ACTIVE CORD AND A CENTER CORD.

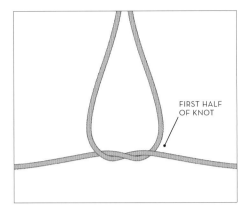

FIRST HALF OF KNOT

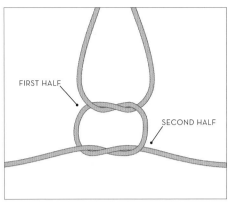

FIRST HALF

SECOND HALF

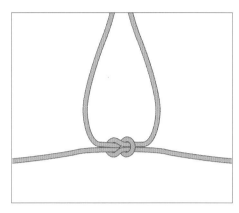

1 Lay the left cord over the right, then pass it under the right cord and up through the opening between them. Pull both cords evenly in opposite directions to tighten. (It is not tightened in the next step so you can see both halves clearly.)

2 The second half is a reverse of the first half. Lay the right cord over the left, then pass it under the left cord and up through the opening between them.

3 Pull both cords equally in opposite directions to tighten the knot.

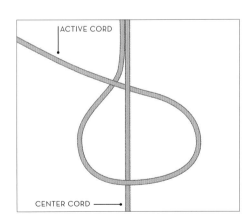

ACTIVE CORD

CENTER CORD

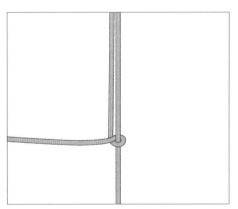

1 Pull the center cord taut and begin with the active cord on the left. Lay the active cord over the center cord, leaving an opening between them on the left side. Thread the active cord under the center cord from the right and up through the opening on the left.

2 Pull the active cord tight to complete the knot.

SPANISH RING KNOT

THIS KNOT IS WIDELY PRAISED AS DECORATIVE AND IS OFTEN USED TO BIND A BUNDLE OF CORDS TOGETHER.

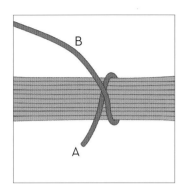

1 Label the cord ends end A (end A is the fixed end) and end B, making sure that end B is on top of end A.

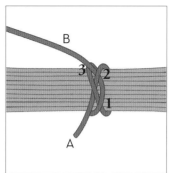

2 Wrap end B around the leather cords, placing it over at point 1, through at point 2, and over at point 3.

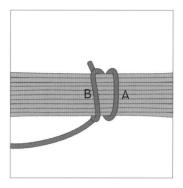

3 Turn the leather cords over, so that end A is on the right-hand side and end B is on the left-hand side.

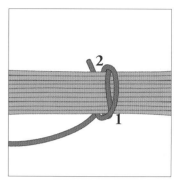

4 Move end B over end A so that the cords overlap at points 1 and 2.

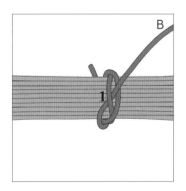

5 Place end B under the left cord and through the opening at point 1.

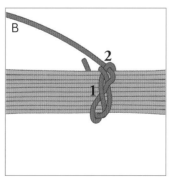

6 Then, place end B under the right cord and through the opening at point 2.

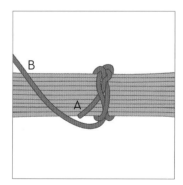

7 Turn the leather cords back over. Ends A and B are now back in their original positions.

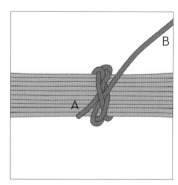

8 Take end B under the left cord and through the opening at end A to complete the knot.

FLAT KNOT
(TO ATTACH LEATHER CORDS TO AN OBJECT)

THIS FLAT KNOT IS USED TO ATTACH THE LEATHER CORDS TO AN OBJECT, SUCH AS A KEY RING.

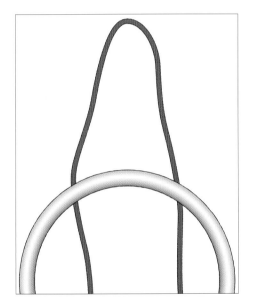

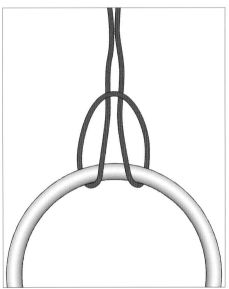

1 Loop the leather cord and place it behind the object. Make sure the loose ends of the cord are below the object and the loop is above it, as shown.

2 Bring the two loose ends up and over the object and thread them through the loop.

3 Tighten the leather cords to fix them securely to the object.

FINISHING FLAT KNOT

THIS FLAT KNOT IS USED TO FINISH A PROJECT BY TYING UP THE LEATHER CORDS.

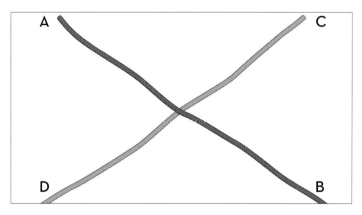

1 Place the red leather cord on top of the green leather cord, as shown. The ends of the red cord are ends A and B and the ends of the green cord are ends C and D.

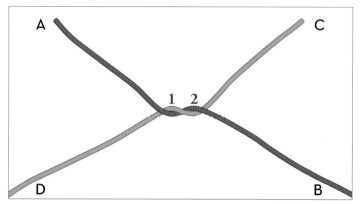

2 Bring end B of the red leather cord under the green leather cord at point 1 and then over it at point 2.

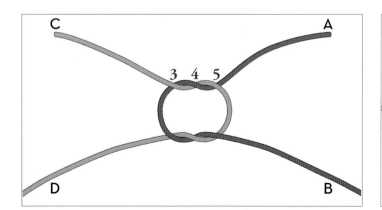

3 Bring ends A and C together. Twist the red and green leather cords around each other once more, as you did in Step 2, but this time wrap end A around end C by passing it under at point 3, over at point 4, and under at point 5.

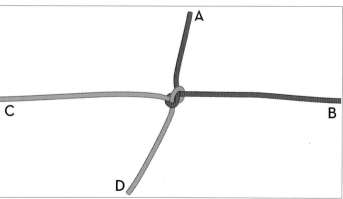

4 Pull ends A and C tight to form a flat knot. Trim the ends of the cords to finish.

FINISHING KNOT

HERE WE ARE USING A RING SIZER TO DEMONSTRATE THIS SIMPLE KNOT, BUT YOU MAY USE IT TO FINISH OFF A WRAPPED OBJECT (SUCH AS A LEATHER RING), A SINGLE CORD, OR A GROUP OF CORDS.

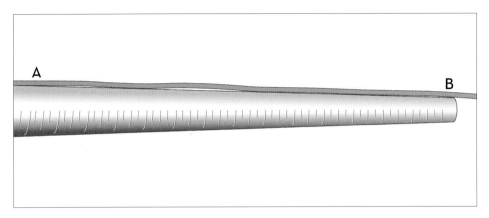

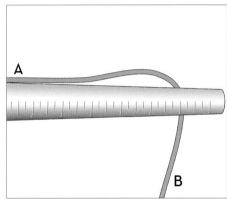

1 Lay the leather cord horizontally alongside the object. Label the ends of the cord end A and end B. End A is the starting end and end B is the expanding end. Tape end A to the object, to keep it firmly in place.

2 Take end B behind the object.

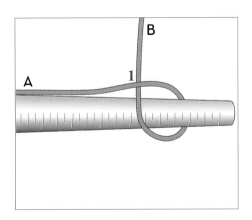

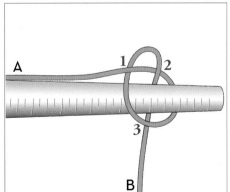

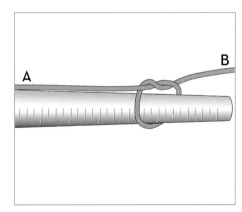

3 Bring end B up and over the object to form a loop, taking it under itself at point 1 to create an overlap.

4 Take end B down through the loop you created in Step 3, forming an overlap at point 2. Then bring end B behind the object and under the loop at point 3.

5 Pull ends A and B to tighten the knot. Trim end B of the cord to finish.

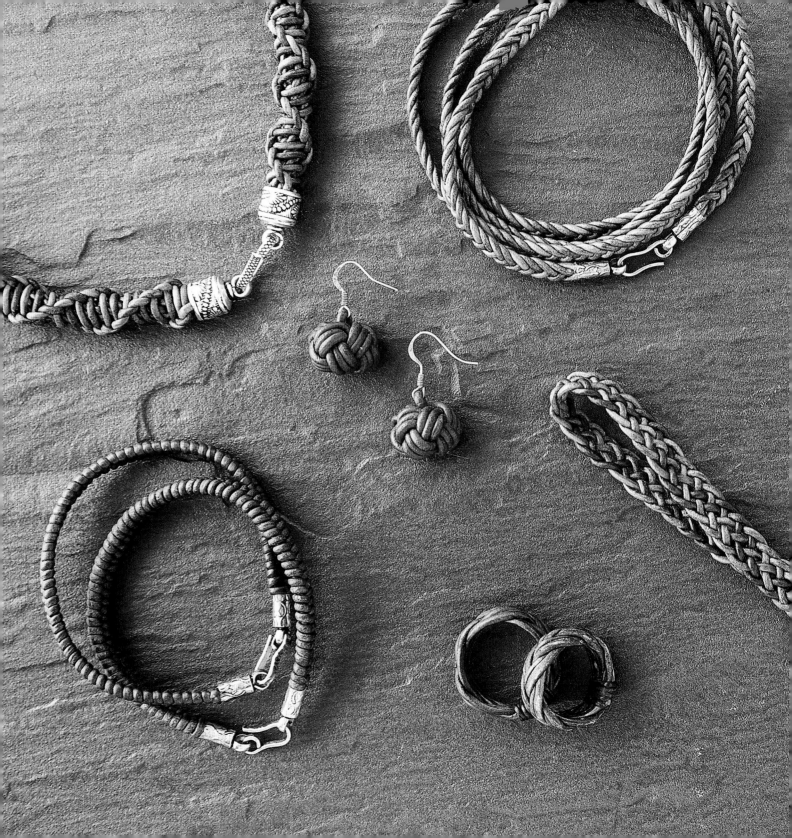

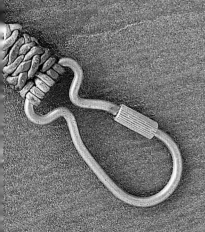

CHAPTER 2
THE PROJECTS

PROJECT FINDER

THIS CHAPTER FEATURES 20 PROJECTS FOR MAKING LEATHER JEWELRY, FROM EARRINGS AND WRIST WEAR TO PENDANTS AND NECKLACES.

WEAVER'S HEART RING   **PAGE 28**

RED LEE BRACELET   **PAGE 32**

MAGNOLIA COIL WRIST WEAR   **PAGE 52**

SIMPLE BRAID WRIST WEAR   **PAGE 56**

BRASS SPRING RING LANYARD   **PAGE 76**

FISH KEY RING   **PAGE 80**

MAGIC BROOM PENDANT   **PAGE 84**

DESERT MOON LEATHER COIL EARRINGS   **PAGE 88**

BRONZE RING PENDANT   **PAGE 36**

INFINITY KNOT WRIST WEAR   **PAGE 40**

WESTERN TASSEL WRIST WEAR   **PAGE 44**

INK-GREEN BRAID WRIST WEAR   **PAGE 48**

SIX-STRING WRIST WEAR   **PAGE 60**

EIGHT-STRING NECKWEAR   **PAGE 64**

ALL-LEATHER ADJUSTABLE NECKLACE
PAGE 68

SIX-STRING WRAP NECKLACE   **PAGE 72**

RIVER BREEZE DOUBLE KNOT EARRINGS
PAGE 92

RED LANTERN EARRINGS   **PAGE 96**

BELT BUCKLE   **PAGE 100**

WRAPPED HANDLE   **PAGE 104**

WEAVER'S HEART RING

THIS STRIKING TWO-COLOR RING IS FORMED USING THE SPANISH RING KNOT (SEE *BASIC TECHNIQUES*, PAGE 20).

TOOLS

Measuring tape

Scissors

Ring sizer

MATERIALS

1 x 35-in. (89-cm) length of 2-mm blue round leather cord

1 x 35-in. (89-cm) length of 2-mm red round leather cord

1 x 15-in. (38-cm) length of 0.5-mm black round leather cord

1 Take the blue leather cord and wrap it around the ring sizer at the desired ring-size mark. Make sure that end B is on top of end A. End A is the fixed end in this project and you will use end B to braid the ring.

2 Wrap end B around the ring sizer, placing it over at point 1, through at point 2, and over at point 3.

3 Turn the ring sizer over, so that end A is on the right-hand side and end B is on the left-hand side.

4 Move end B over end A so that the cords overlap at points 1 and 2.

5 Place end B under the left cord and through the opening at point 1, and then under the right cord and through the opening at point 2.

6 Turn the ring sizer back over again. Ends A and B are now back in their original positions. Take end B under the left cord and through the opening at end A to complete the circular braid. Steps 1–6 complete the Spanish Ring Knot (see *Basic Techniques*, page 20).

7 Place the red leather cord through the opening formed between ends A and B, and follow the path you made with the blue leather cord to circle the ring sizer once. Remove the ring from the ring sizer. Soak the ring in lukewarm water, let air-dry for 30 minutes, and then trim off the excess cords.

8 Place the black leather cord through the opening formed where end A meets end B.

9 Wrap the black leather cord neatly around the ring until you can no longer see the ends of A and B. To complete the ring, make a Finishing Knot (see *Basic Techniques*, page 23).

TIP: For more on the Spanish Ring Knot method of braiding, see page 390 of Bruce Grant's *Encyclopedia of Rawhide and Leather Braiding*.

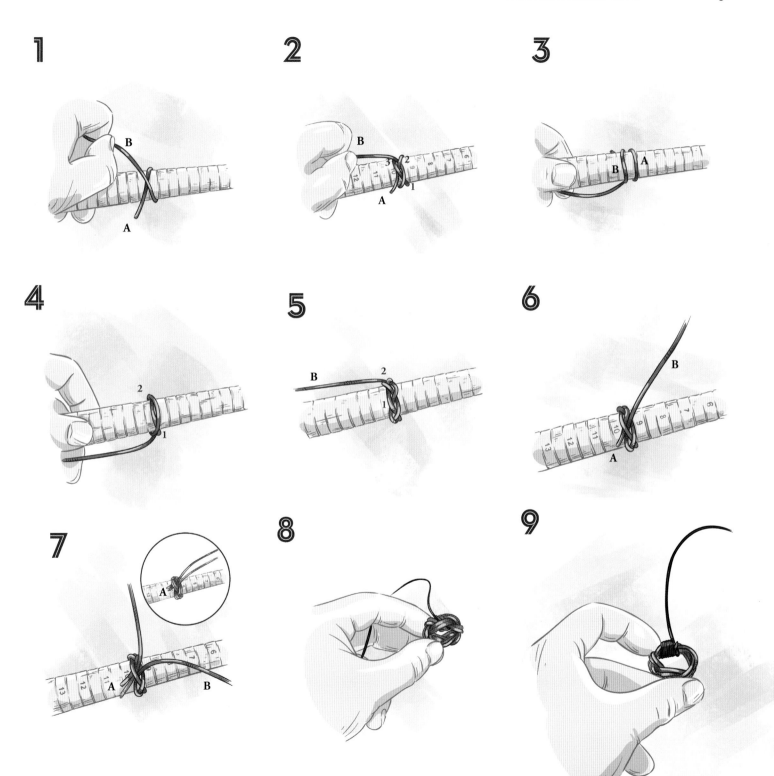

RED LEE BRACELET

THIS WRIST PIECE HAS A REALLY PLEASING MIX OF TEXTURES, WITH A CHUNKY BRAID WRAPPED TIGHTLY IN A FINER, MORE DELICATE CORD. A PAIR OF INTRICATELY DECORATED RED COPPER ENDS ADD A BEAUTIFUL FINISH TO THIS RUSTIC BRACELET.

TOOLS

Measuring tape

Scissors

Glue

MATERIALS

4 x 10-in. (25-cm) lengths of 4-mm natural brown round leather cords

2 x 36-in. (92-cm) lengths of 1.5-mm natural red round leather cords

10-mm glue-on clasps

Note: The materials indicated are for a bracelet 7-in. (18-cm) long. If you would like it to be longer, increase the length of the cords to your liking.

1 Place a 1.5-mm red leather cord in the middle of four 4-mm brown leather cords. Hold the cords together at the top, then 1½-in. (4-cm) down, pull the red leather cord out from the center and start coiling it around the four brown leather cords. Because leather is elastic, make sure to stretch the red leather cord and coil it as tightly as possible to prevent it from loosening.

2 Coil the red leather cord for a length of 1½-in. (4-cm). Knot by wrapping the cord under, then over itself, and pulling tight.

3 Once you have made the knot, cut off any extra red cord.

4 In order to start braiding the brown leather cords, spread them out from left to right. The cords are labeled A to D, with A on the far left and D on the far right.

5 First take cord D, pass it over cord C toward cord B, and make it parallel to cord B. Then take cord A, pass it over cord B toward cord C, and make it parallel to cord C.

6 Take cord C, pass it over cord A toward cord D, and make it parallel to cord D. Take cord B, pass it over cord D toward cord A, and make it parallel to cord A. Continue braiding by repeating Steps 5 and 6 for 3-in. (8-cm).

7 Insert the red leather cord in between the four brown leather cords at the other end of the bracelet and start coiling around the four brown leather cords for 1½-in. (4-cm).

8 Knot the red leather as described in Step 2 and cut off the excess.

9 Place a drop of glue into the glue-on clasps and insert the knotted ends into the clasps. Wait at least two hours for the glue to dry.

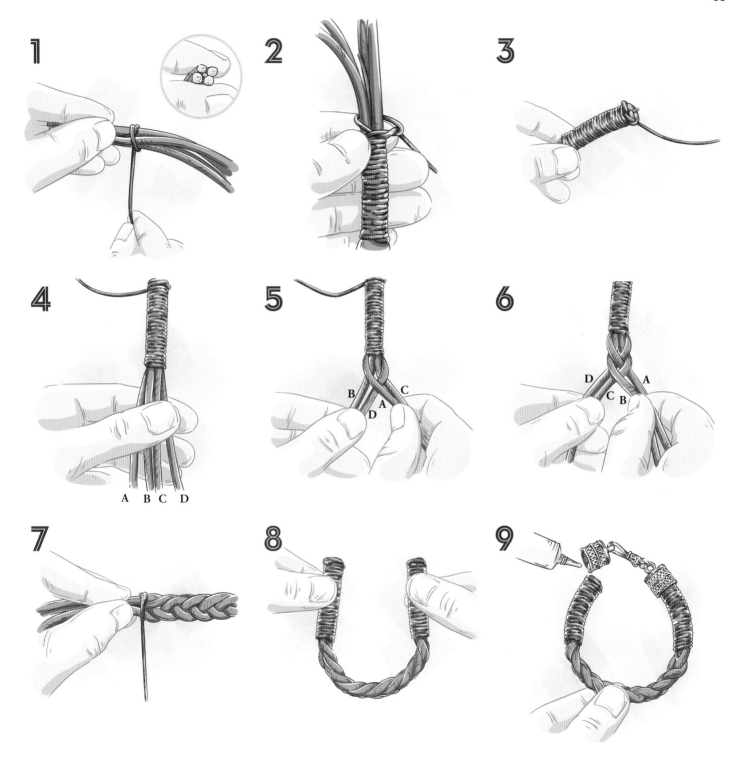

BRONZE RING PENDANT

THE BRONZE RING USED TO MAKE THIS PENDANT IS A DRAPE RING FROM THE 1960s. THE PENDANT IS CREATED USING THE HALF-HITCH KNOT (SEE *BASIC TECHNIQUES*, PAGE 19) TO WRAP A 1-MM ROUND LEATHER CORD AROUND THE RING AND FORM A SPIRAL PATTERN. THIS PENDANT IS RETRO AND MYSTERIOUS, AND CAN BE HUNG ANYWHERE YOU LIKE.

TOOLS

Measuring tape

Scissors

MATERIALS

Vintage bronze ring (such as an old drape ring)

1 x 55-in. (140-cm) length of 1-mm natural dark brown round leather cord

1 Wrap the leather cord around the bronze ring once, as shown. The starting point for the braiding is end A and the expanding end is end B.

2 Take end B and wrap it once around the bronze ring at point 1. This is the starting point for the Half-Hitch Knot (see *Basic Techniques*, page 19).

3 Take end B and wrap it once around the bronze ring and through at point 2. This is the complete Half-Hitch Knot and the repeating step for creating the braid.

4 Repeat Step 3 until the bronze ring is completely covered with cord. When braiding, leather cord can be rather flexible, so be aware of how tightly you are wrapping it around the ring. Ensure that the braid is neither too tight nor too loose.

5 Take the extra lengths of end A and end B, and make two Finishing Flat Knots (see *Basic Techniques*, page 22). To finish, trim off the excess cords

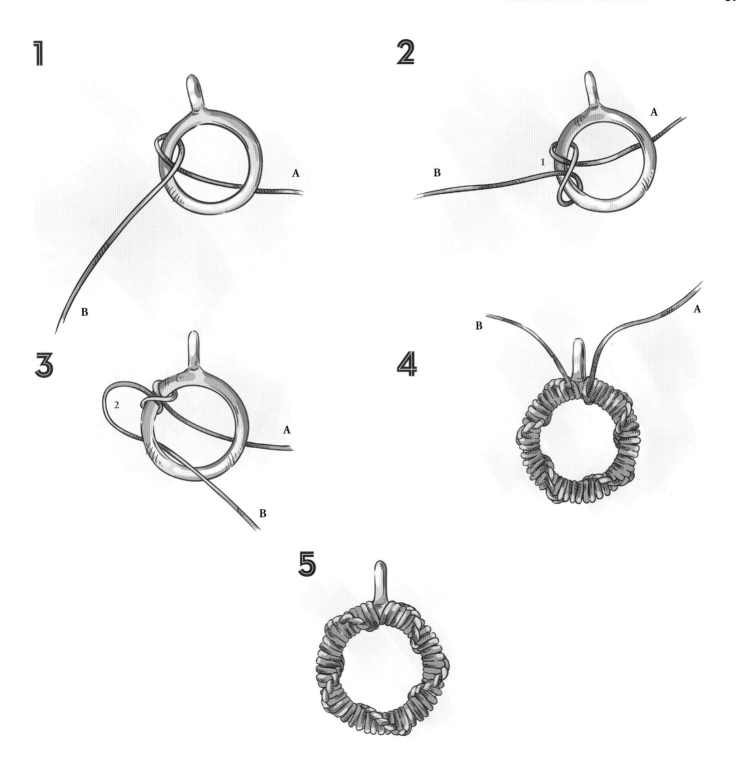

INFINITY KNOT WRIST WEAR

THIS ALL-LEATHER WRIST WEAR IS VERY EASY TO MAKE. IT IS PERFECT FOR BEGINNERS WHO WOULD LIKE TO CREATE A SPECIAL HANDMADE GIFT FOR A LOVED ONE.

TOOLS

Measuring tape

Scissors

MATERIALS

1 x 20-in. (50-cm) length of 4-mm round
leather cord

Note: The length of leather cord you
will need to make this bracelet is the desired
circumference of the bracelet + 12-in. (30-cm).

1 Make a knot in the cord at end A,
as shown.

2 Take end B and thread it through the
opening in the end A knot. Create a
loop, then tighten the end A knot. This is
the female end of a set of coupling ends.
The size of the opening at the female end
can be adjusted by pulling on end B.

3 After adjusting the opening of the
female end to the desired size, make
another knot 3-in. (8-cm) from the end
A knot.

4 Take end B and thread it through the
opening in the newly made knot,
leaving an opening with a diameter of
4-mm (i.e., approximately the thickness of
the leather cord).

5 Take end B and thread it upward
through the back of the 4-mm
opening, creating another opening on
the right.

6 Twist the last opening you made
upward to create another opening
with a diameter of 4-mm.

7 Take end B and thread it through the
4-mm opening you just made.

8 Overlap end B, as shown, to create a
small opening.

9 Preserving the opening, bring the
loose end of B down over the front
of the leather cord, then thread it through
the B opening on the right. This is the
other end—the male end—of the
coupling end, for fastening the bracelet.

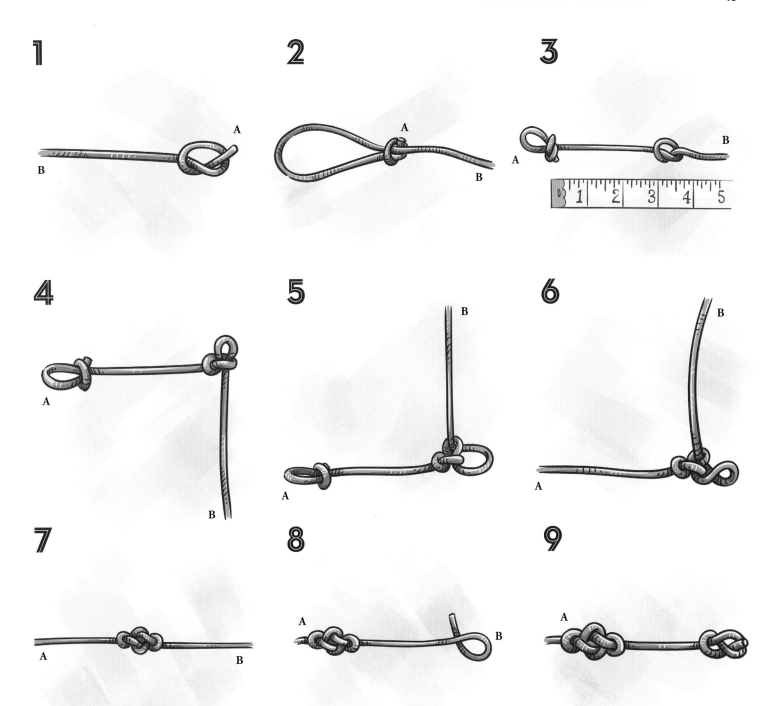

WESTERN TASSEL WRIST WEAR

THIS WRIST WEAR ONLY REQUIRES THREE LENGTHS OF LEATHER CORD AND IS A VERY GOOD EXAMPLE OF HOW TO MAKE A PIECE OF JEWELRY USING ONLY LEATHER CORDS.

TOOLS

Measuring tape

Scissors

MATERIALS

1 x 60-in. (152-cm) length of 1.5-mm natural round leather cord

1 x 40-in. (102-cm) length of 1.5-mm natural gray round leather cord

1 x 40-in. (102-cm) length of 1.5-mm natural brown round leather cord

1 In this project, the three leather cords are treated as one cord. Align the three leather cords at one end. Wrap end A of the cords over your left index finger, leaving a length of 20-in. (50-cm). Make a loop with end B, as shown, and place this on top of the cords on your finger.

2 Take end A of the leather cords, then loop them through as one strand under at point 1, over at point 2, under at point 3, and at over point 4.

3 Take end B of the leather cords and bring it counterclockwise to loop under at point 1 and through the center of point 2.

4 Take end A of the leather cords and bring it counterclockwise to go under at point 1 and through the center of point 2.

5 Tighten ends A and B of the cords. The resulting knot is the starting point for the piece of wrist wear. You now have six strands of leather cord to braid with.

6 The six leather cords will be braided in double working strands. Simply divide the six strands of cord into three groups. From left to right, these are labeled C, D, and E.

7 To braid the cords, fold group C inward (i.e., toward the middle) and place it between groups D and E. Then fold group E inward and place it between groups D and C. This completes the three-strand braid pattern. Repeat this pattern until the braiding reaches the desired length (in this case, 10-in./25-cm).

8 Make a loop with end B, roughly the same size as the knot in Step 5. Leave approximately 1-in. (2.5-cm) of extra braid for overlapping.

9 Take the longest leather cord and wrap it neatly around the five other loose cords and the braided leather cords. Keep wrapping until the loop at end B is barely large enough to fit over the knot. To finish, make a Finishing Knot (see *Basic Techniques*, page 23).

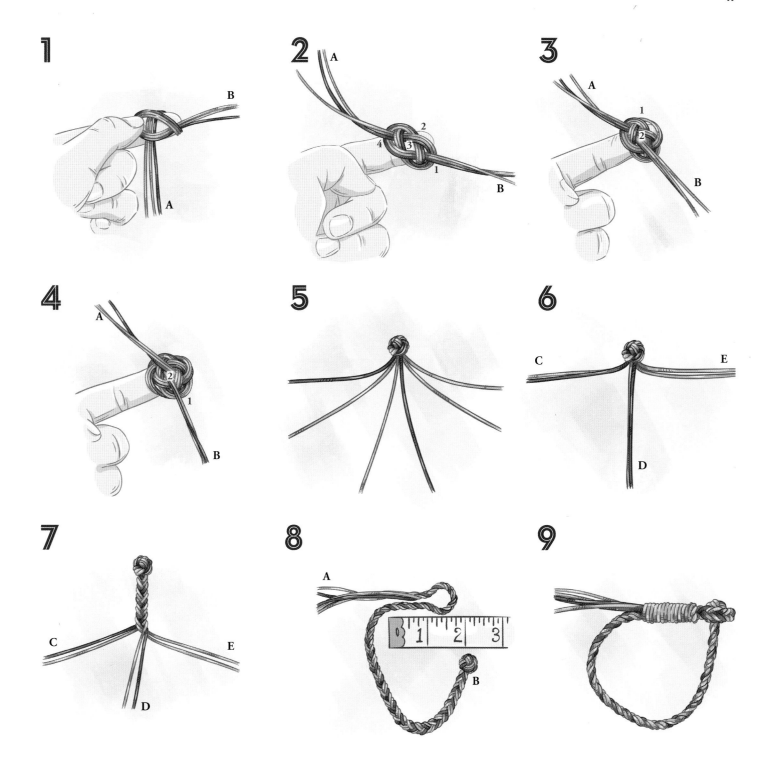

INK-GREEN BRAID WRIST WEAR

THIS IS A BEAUTIFUL PIECE OF WRIST WEAR THAT IS SUITABLE FOR BOTH MEN AND WOMEN. THE THICKNESS OF THE LEATHER CORDS DETERMINES BOTH THE THICKNESS AND WIDTH OF THE STYLE.

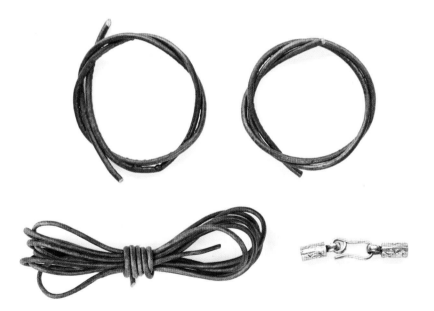

TOOLS

Measuring tape

Scissors

Glue

MATERIALS

4-mm metal glue-on clasp

2 x 12-in. (30-cm) lengths of 2-mm blue round leather cord

1 x 80-in. (203-cm) length of 1½-mm green round leather cord

1 Glue one end of the two blue leather cords and the green leather cord into the "hook" part of the metal clasp.

2 Position the green leather cord so that it is in between the two blue leather cords. Designate the blue cord on the left as A and the blue cord on the right as B.

3 Loop the green cord around cords B and A by going under cord B and over cord A to form a circle.

4 After making the loop with the green leather cord, position it in the middle of the two blue leather cords. This is the starting point of the braiding.

5 Wrap the green leather cord around blue cord B.

6 Wrap the green leather cord around blue cord A, creating an infinity symbol. When wrapping, make sure that the green cord is wrapped tightly around the blue cords and that the blue cords do not show from underneath.

7 Keep making infinity loops with the green leather cord until you reach the desired length of the bracelet. Remember to leave enough length (approximately ³⁄₁₆-in./5-mm) of leather cords for gluing into the other part of the clasp. Trim off the excess leather cords.

8 Glue the ends of the leather cords into the "eye" part of the metal clasp and let dry for 24 hours.

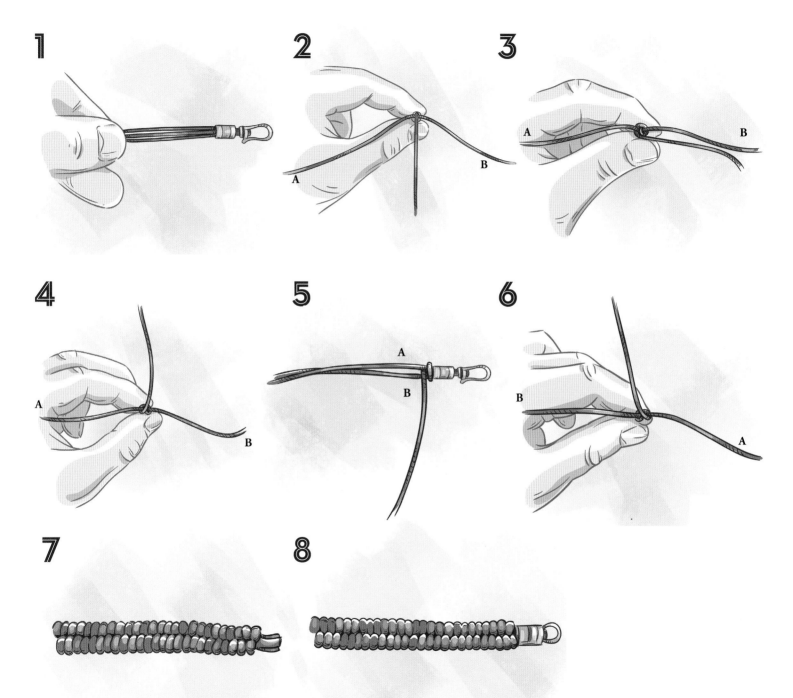

MAGNOLIA COIL WRIST WEAR

THIS SIMPLE PIECE OF WRIST WEAR, WITH ITS ATTRACTIVE COPPER CLASP, IS VERY EASY TO MAKE.

TOOLS

Measuring tape

Scissors

Glue

MATERIALS

4-mm metal glue-on clasp

3 x 12-in. (30-cm) lengths of 1.5-mm natural blue round leather cord

1 x 65-in. (165-cm) length of 1.5-mm natural brown round leather cord

1 Glue one end of the four leather cords into the "hook" part of the metal clasps.

2 Wrap the brown leather cord tightly around the three blue leather cords. The key to success in this project is managing the tension as you coil the brown cord. Each coil should be wrapped tightly around the three blue leather cords, and the blue leather cords should not be visible.

3 Keep coiling the brown leather cord around the blue leather cords until you reach the desired length of the bracelet. This bracelet is 8-in. (20-cm) in length.

4 Trim off the excess leather cords, leaving approximately ³⁄₁₆-in. (5-mm) of the cords unwrapped for gluing into the other part of the clasp.

5 Glue the ends of the leather cords into the "eye" part of the clasp and let dry for 24 hours.

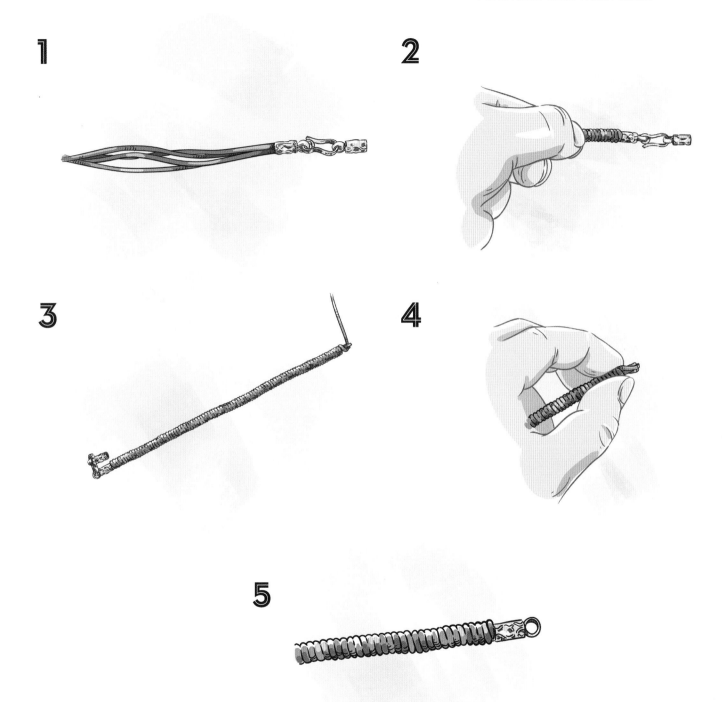

SIMPLE BRAID WRIST WEAR

THE TOTAL FINISHED LENGTH OF THIS WRAP-AROUND WRIST WEAR IS APPROXIMATELY 35-IN. (89-CM). THIS LENGTH CAN BE WRAPPED AROUND THE WRIST FOUR TIMES. A SINGLE LOOP OF THE BRACELET MEASURES ABOUT 7-IN. (18-CM). IT IS MADE WITH COLORFUL LEATHER CORDS.

TOOLS

Measuring tape

Scissors

Glue

MATERIALS

4-mm metal glue-on clasp

2 x 50-in. (127-cm) lengths of 1.5-mm natural blue round leather cord

1 x 50-in. (127-cm) length of 1.5-mm natural brown round leather cord

1 x 50-in. (127-cm) length of 1.5-mm natural gray round leather cord

1 Glue one end of the four leather cords into the "hook" part of the clasp.

2 Separate the four leather cords. From left to right, designate these A, B, C, and D. Cord A is gray, cord B is brown, and cords C and D are both blue.

3 To start braiding, place cord A over cord B, as shown.

4 Place cord D over cords C and A. This is a finished braiding pattern. Redesignate the cords in order, from left to right, as follows: cord A (brown), cord B (blue), cord C (gray), and cord D (blue).

5 Repeat Steps 3 and 4, placing cord A over cord B and then cord D over cords C and A. Redesignate the order of the cords once more. Keep braiding and redesignating the cords in this way until you reach the desired length for the bracelet (in this case, 35-in./89-cm).

6 Trim off the excess leather cords, leaving approximately 3/16-in. (5-mm) of unbraided cords for gluing into the other part of the clasp.

7 Glue the ends of the leather cords into the "eye" part of the clasp.

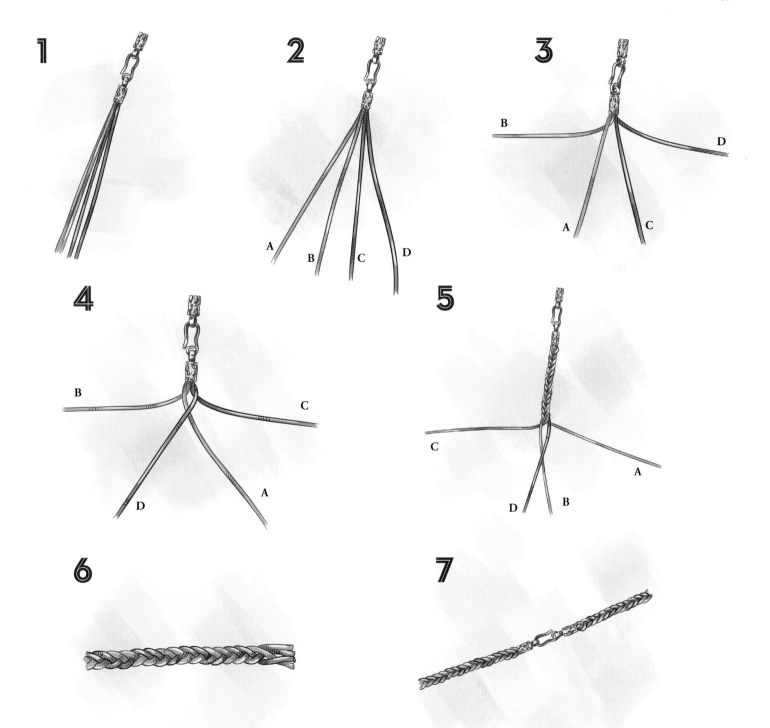

SIX=STRING WRIST WEAR

THIS WRIST WEAR CAN BE WORN BY BOTH MEN AND WOMEN. ALTHOUGH THE BRAIDED PATTERN LOOKS VERY SIMPLE, WE ALTERED THE DIRECTION OF THE BRAIDING FOR ONE OF THE SETS OF CORDS AND THE PATTERN CHANGED QUITE DRASTICALLY. WE HOPE THAT THIS EXPERIMENTATION WILL ENCOURAGE YOU TO EXPERIMENT, TOO, AS YOU DISCOVER THE JOYS OF BRAIDING LEATHER.

TOOLS

Measuring tape

Scissors

Glue

MATERIALS

4.5-mm metal glue-on clasp

2 x 15-in. (38-cm) lengths of 1.5-mm natural red round leather cord

2 x 15-in. (38-cm) lengths of 1.5-mm natural green round leather cord

2 x 15-in. (38-cm) lengths of 1.5-mm natural brown round leather cord

1 Glue one end of the six leather cords into the "hook" part of the metal clasp. Divide the six cords randomly into three groups. Designate these groups A, B, and C.

2 Place group C over group B, placing it in between group A and group B.

3 Switch over the position of the cords in group A, then place group A in between group C and group B.

4 Place group B between group A and group C, but without switching over the position of the cords, as you did in Step 3.

5 Switch over the cords in group C, then place group C in between group B and group A.

6 Switch over the cords in group A, then place group A in between group B and group C.

7 Place group B in between groups A and C, again without switching over the cords. Groups A, B, and C are now in their original starting positions.

8 Repeat Steps 2–7, braiding until you reach the desired length of the bracelet. In this example, the length is 8-in. (20-cm), minus the 1½-in. (4-cm) of the metal endings. Trim off the excess leather cords, leaving approximately ³⁄₁₆-in. (5-mm) of unbraided cords for gluing into the other part of the clasp.

9 Glue the ends of the braided cords into the "eye" part of the clasp and let dry for 24 hours.

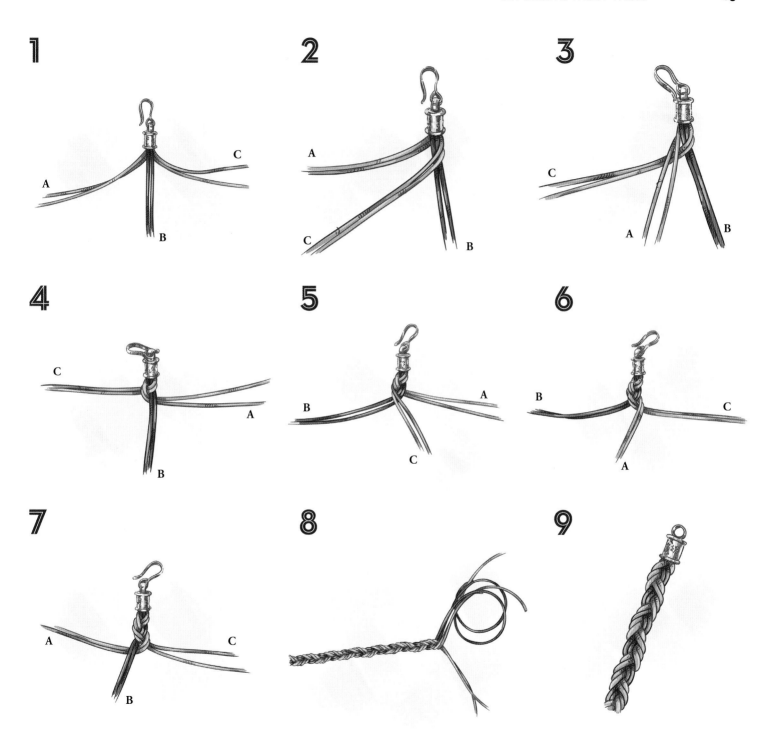

EIGHT-STRING NECKWEAR

THIS NECKWEAR IS CREATED USING A FOUR-STRAND BRAID WHERE TWO OF THE FOUR STRANDS ARE TRIPLED. THE FINISHED BRAIDED NECKLACE RESEMBLES THE WAVES OF THE OCEAN AND IS A VERY FEMININE PIECE.

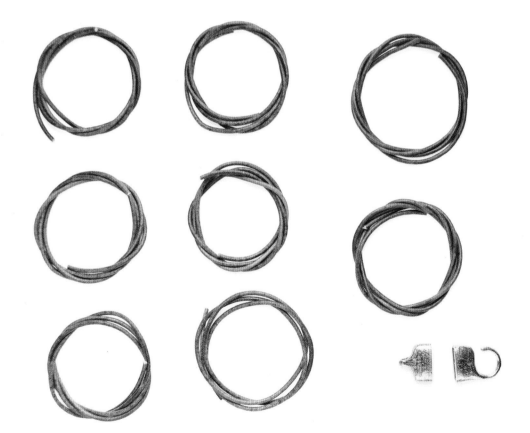

TOOLS

Measuring tape

Scissors

Glue

MATERIALS

16-mm metal glue–on clasp

6 x 20-in. (50-cm) lengths of 2-mm natural gray round leather cord

2 x 25-in. (64-cm) lengths of 2-mm natural green round leather cord

1 Glue the eight leather cords into the "hook" part of the metal clasp. From left to right, designate these cords A to H. Place the green cords at positions D and E.

2 Bring cord D to the left, so that it is sitting behind cords A, B, and C. Bring cord E to the right, so that it is on top of cords F, G, and H.

3 Without changing the position of the green cords D and E in any way, place cords F, G, and H over cords A, B, and C.

4 Place cord D on top of cords F, G, and H. Place cord E behind cords A, B, and C, then on top of cord D.

5 Place cords F, G, and H on top of cord E, then place cords A, B, and C on top of cords F, G, and H.

6 Place cord E on top of cords A, B, and C. Place cord D behind cords F, G, and H, then on top of cord E.

7 Repeat Steps 2–7, braiding until you reach the desired length. Trim off the excess leather cords, leaving approximately 3/16-in. (5-mm) of unbraided cords for gluing into the other part of the clasp.

8 Glue the ends of the braided cords into the "eye" part of the clasp and let dry for 24 hours.

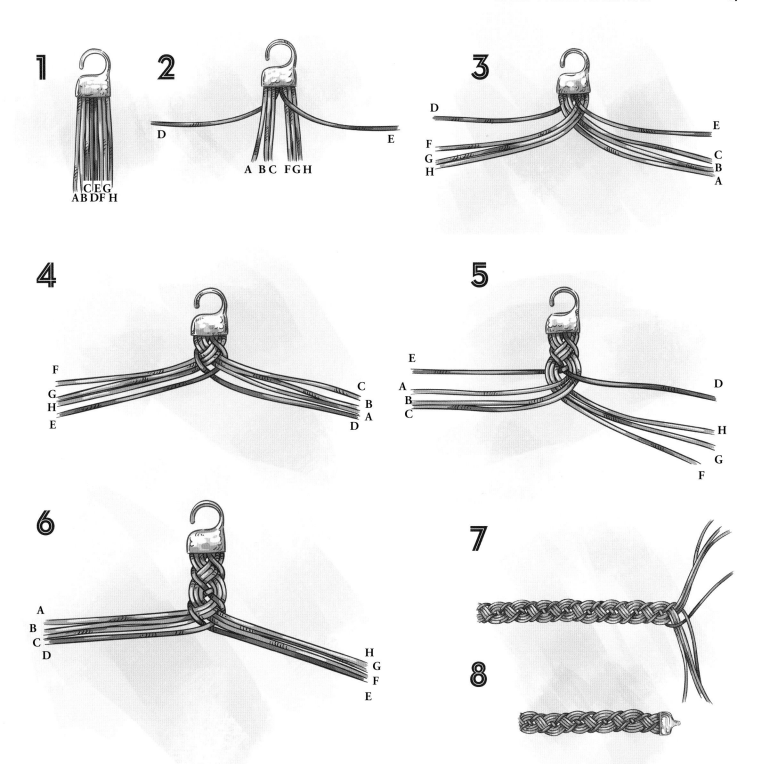

ALL-LEATHER ADUSTABLE NECKLACE

THIS NECKLACE HAS A VERY PRACTICAL DESIGN. A LENGTH OF LEATHER CORD AND TWO KNOTS CREATE A NECKLACE WITH A 19- TO 37-IN. (48- TO 94-CM) ADJUSTABLE OPENING. THIS IS A BASIC NECKLACE THAT CAN BE WORN WITH OTHER PENDANTS, SUCH AS THE MAGIC BROOM PENDANT (PAGE 84) AND BRONZE RING PENDANT (PAGE 36).

TOOLS

Measuring tape

Scissors

MATERIALS

1 x 50-in. (20-cm) length of 4-mm natural dark brown round leather cord

1 Choose one end of the leather cord to be end A and the other to be end B. Fold end A in by 6-in. (15-cm). Designate the second string resulting from this fold as end C.

2 Bring end B counterclockwise and position it, as shown, so that it is the same length as end A. Designate the resulting fold on the left as end D.

3 One-inch (2.5-cm) from end D, take end A and wrap it three times around ends A, B, and C, then through the opening at end D.

4 Pull the leather cord at end C, tighten the knot, and trim off the extra leather cord. At the same time, allow the leather cord at end B to move through the opening in the knot. Be careful not to trim off too much leather cord at end A or to tighten the knot too much. It is best when end B can still be moved with a slight effort.

5 Pull on end B of the cord so that it passes through the knot and reaches a length of 12-in. (30-cm).

6 Use the method described in Steps 2–4 to create another knot, taking the leather cord at end B and wrapping it around end C.

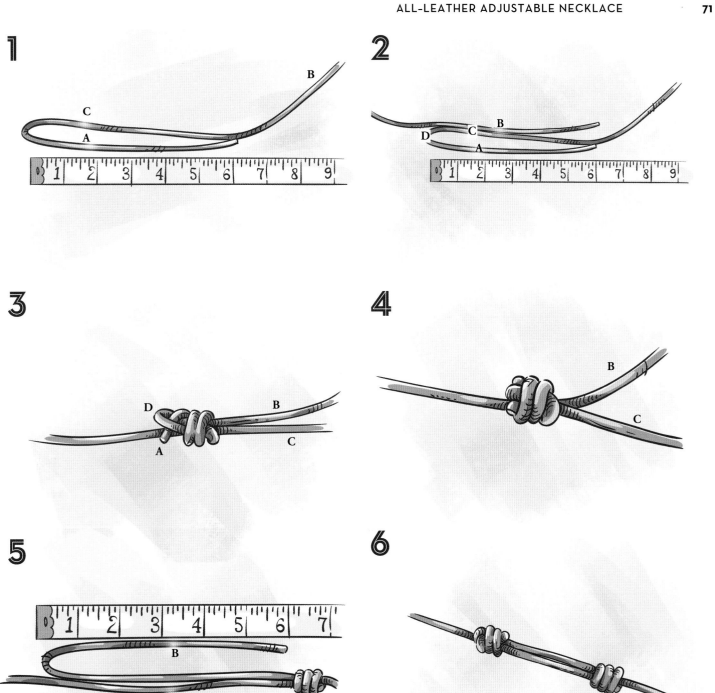

SIX=STRING WRAP NECKLACE

THIS NECKWEAR CAN BE WORN BY BOTH MEN AND WOMEN. FROM A TECHNIQUE POINT OF VIEW, THIS PROJECT REQUIRES MORE TIME AND EFFORT, AS WELL AS LOTS OF LEATHER CORDS. HOWEVER, THE RESULTING BRAIDS ARE RICH IN TEXTURE AND PATTERN, AND THE FINISHED NECKLACE HAS A PLEASING THREE-DIMENSIONAL QUALITY.

TOOLS

Measuring tape

Scissors

Short piece of string

Glue

MATERIALS

8-mm glue-on clasp

4 x 60-in. (152-cm) lengths of 1-mm natural blue round leather cord

1 x 90-in. (229-cm) length of 1.5-mm natural green round leather cord

1 x 90-in. (229-cm) length of 1.5-mm natural brown round leather cord

1 Lay the four lengths of blue leather cord alongside the measuring tape. Tie a short piece of string around the four cords at the 3-in. (7.5-cm) mark.

2 Designate the cords A, B, C, and D. Place cord A under cord B, place cord B under cord C, place cord C under cord D, and then take cord D under cord A.

3 Weave cord D through the opening behind point 1. Weave cord A through the opening behind point 2. Weave cord B through the opening behind point 3. Weave cord C through the opening behind point 4.

4 Pull cords A, B, C, and D until they no longer move.

5 Using this knot as your starting point, repeat Steps 2–4 until you reach the desired length of the braid. In this example, the length of the braid is 14-in. (35.5-cm).

6 Stabilize the cords to finish the main body. Glue the main body of the necklace and also the 1.5-mm green and brown cords into the "hook" part of the metal clasp. Make sure the two 1.5-mm cords are on the left- and right-hand sides of the main body.

7 Wrap the brown cord behind the main body of the necklace. Take the green cord and bring it under the brown cord on the left-hand side of the main body. Wrap the green cord halfway around the main body and then weave it through the loop in the brown cord on the right-hand side. This is the start of a Square Knot (see *Basic Techniques*, page 19).

8 Take the green cord and bring it behind the main body. Take the brown cord and bring it behind the green cord on the left-hand side of the main body. Wrap the brown cord halfway around the main body and then weave it through the loop in the green cord on the right-hand side. This is the finished Square Knot.

9 Repeat Steps 7–8 until the main body is wrapped in the green and brown cords. Trim off the excess cords, leaving about $3/16$-in. (5-mm) unbraided for gluing into the other metal ending. Glue the cords into the "eye" part of the clasp and let dry for 24 hours.

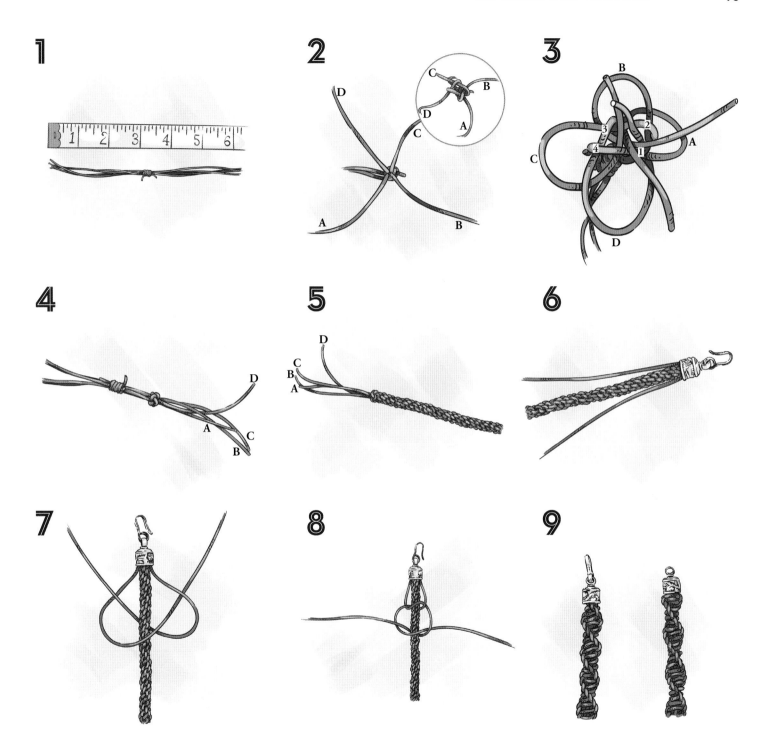

BRASS SPRING RING LANYARD

THIS PROJECT IS A FORM OF LONG NECKWEAR. YOU CAN USE THE VINTAGE CLASP TO HANG KEYS, WORK BADGES, OR EVEN A CELLPHONE.

TOOLS

Measuring tape

Scissors

MATERIALS

1 x 18- to 22-mm diameter vintage brass spring ring clasp

4 x 50-in. (127-cm) lengths of 1.5-mm natural brown round leather cord

2 x 50-in. (127-cm) lengths of 1.5-mm natural gray round leather cord

1 Thread two of the brown leather cords and one of the gray leather cords onto the ring clasp. Fold the cords in half so that the clasp is sitting in the middle of the three cords. You now have six cords to work with. Starting on the left and moving counterclockwise, designate the cords A to F.

2 Take cord A under cord B at point 6, take cord B under cord C at point 1, take cord C under cord D at point 2, take cord D under cord E at point 3, take cord E under cord F at point 4, then take cord F under cord A at point 5.

3 Tighten cords A to F. Weave cord A under at point 1, cord B under at point 2, cord C under at point 3, cord D under at point 4, cord E under at point 5, and cord F under at point 6.

4 Separate cords A to F. Overlap cords C and D, with cord C going in front and cord D behind.

5 Take cord A and bring it behind cords B, D, and C, then position it in between cords C and D.

6 Take cord F and bring it behind cords E, A, and C. Bring cord F over cord A, then position it in between cords A and C.

7 Now, redesignate the cords in order as A to F, from left to right. Wrap the left-most cord from the back to the front of cord D and place it in between cords C and D. Then wrap the right-most cord from the back to the front of cord C and place it in between cords C and D. Redesignate the cords in order as A to F once more and then repeat the braiding and refreshing process—explained in Steps 4–7—until you reach the desired length of braiding. In this example, the length of braiding is 15-in. (38-cm).

8 Take the remaining two brown leather cords and the gray leather cord and thread them onto the clasp, as you did in Step 1. Repeat Steps 2–7 to create the other side of the lanyard.

9 To finish, overlap the six cords at end A with the six cords at end B, then braid the six cords at end A using the knot technique described in Step 3. Trim off the excess cords.

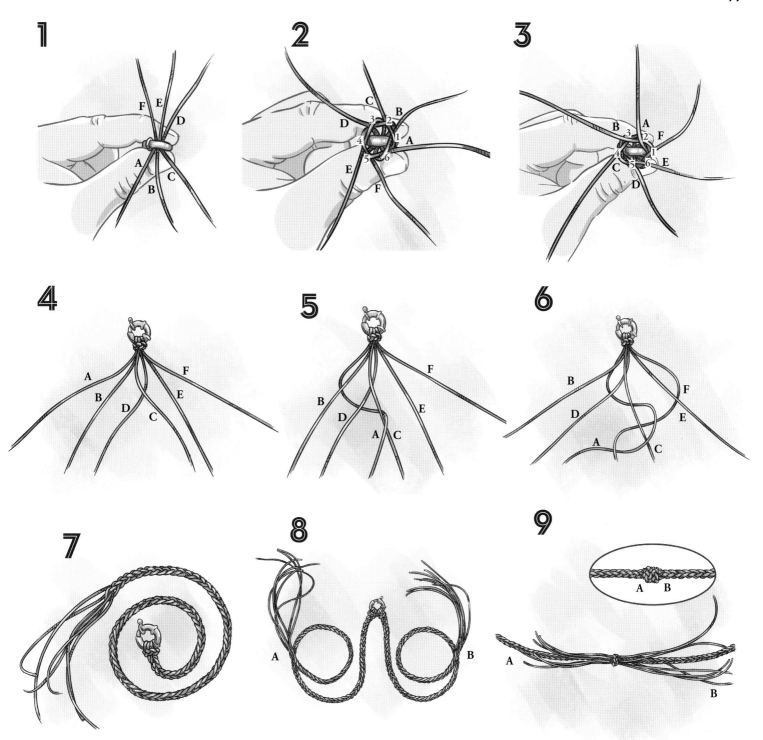

FISH KEY RING

THIS KEY RING IS MADE WITH LEATHER CORDS AND A VINTAGE KEY RING—
THE ONE USED HERE WAS PRODUCED IN THE 1960s. MADE WITH PURE
BRAIDING TECHNIQUES, THIS KEY RING WILL BE CHALLENGING FOR
MOST BEGINNERS.

TOOLS

Measuring tape

Scissors

MATERIALS

Vintage key ring

1 x 35-in. (89-cm) length of 1.5-mm natural gray round leather cord

1 x 35-in. (89-cm) length of 1.5-mm natural dark brown round leather cord

1 x 35-in. (89-cm) length of 1.5-mm natural brown round leather cord

1 Fold one of the leather cords in half. The open end is end B and the curved end is end A.

2 Loop end A through the key ring, as shown, then take end B through the opening in end A and tighten the cords. This attaches the leather cord to the key ring.

3 Attach the other two leather cords to the key ring in the same way as you did in Step 2. You should now have a total of six cords attached to the ring. From left to right, designate these A to F.

4 Place cord A in front of cord B and behind cord C. Place cord F behind cord E and over cord D. Place cord A over cord F. Relabel the cord as A to F, from left to right.

5 Keep repeating Step 4 until you reach the desired length of braiding. In this example, the length is 8-in. (20-cm). Fold the braiding over in the middle.

6 Once you have folded the braid over in the middle, place cords A, B, C, D, E, and F through the openings at points 1, 2, 3, 4, 5, and 6, respectively. Tighten the cords.

7 Wrap cord D around the braided body and the other five cords using the Spanish Ring Knot technique (see *Basic Techniques*, page 20).

8 Wrap cord B around the braided body and the other four cords, creating another Spanish Ring Knot.

9 Wrap cord C around the braided body and the other three cords, again creating a Spanish Ring Knot. To finish, trim off the excess cords.

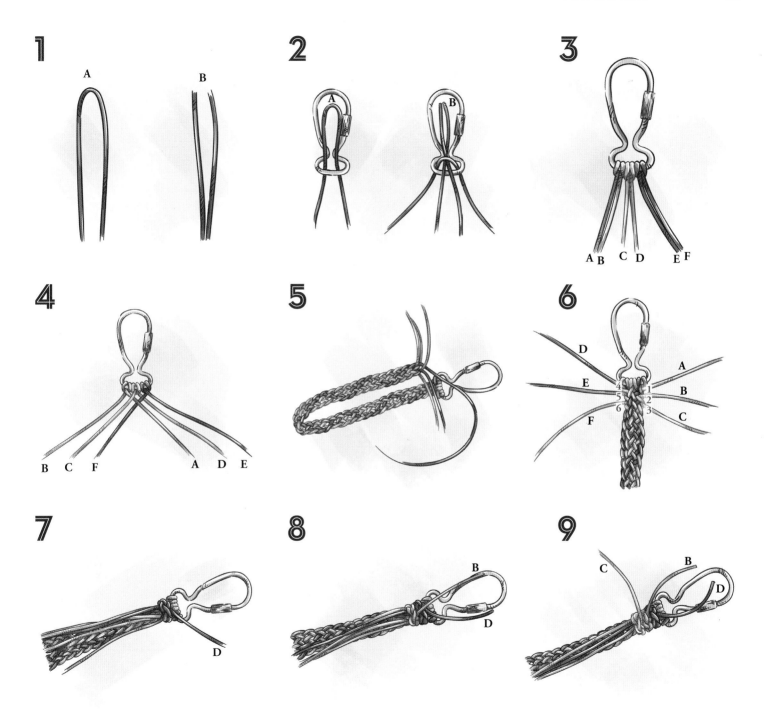

MAGIC BROOM PENDANT

WHEN BRAIDING LEATHER CORDS, IT CAN BE DIFFICULT TO ESTIMATE THE LENGTH OF CORDS NEEDED. AS A RESULT, YOU OFTEN END UP WITH A LOT OF SCRAP CORDS. WHY NOT REUSE AND RECYCLE THEM WITH THIS EASY TO MAKE PROJECT?

TOOLS

Measuring tape

Scissors

2 rubber bands

MATERIALS

Vintage bronze ring

Selection of leather cords in different colors, with lengths over 6-in. (15-cm)

1 x 20-in. (50-cm) length of 0.5-mm natural brown round leather cord

1 x 20 in. (50-cm) length of 2-mm natural blue round leather

1 x 10-in. (25-cm) length of 2-mm natural blue round leather cord

Note: For this project, you need leather cords with lengths over 6-in. (15-cm). No specific colors or thicknesses of cords are required.

1 Lay out your selection of leather cords, as shown, and use one of the rubber bands to gather together the bundle at one end. Designate the neat, even end, end A, and the other end, end B.

2 Take the 0.5-mm brown leather cord and use it to make a Spanish Ring Knot (see *Basic Techniques*, page 20), 2-in. (5-cm) from end A.

3 Fold over all the leather cords at end B toward end A, using the other rubber band to stabilize the bundle of cords.

4 Take the longer of the two blue leather cords and use this to make another Spanish Ring Knot, this time ½-in. (12-mm) from end B. Remove the rubber band that was holding the bundle of cords together.

5 Trim the ends of end A neatly and evenly.

6 Attach the shorter of the two blue leather cords to the ring with a Flat Knot (see *Basic Techniques*, page 21). Feed both ends of this cord through the center of end B, so that they come out at end A, to attach the broom to the ring.

7 Make two Flat Knots with the ends of the shorter blue leather cord at end A, to finish the pendant.

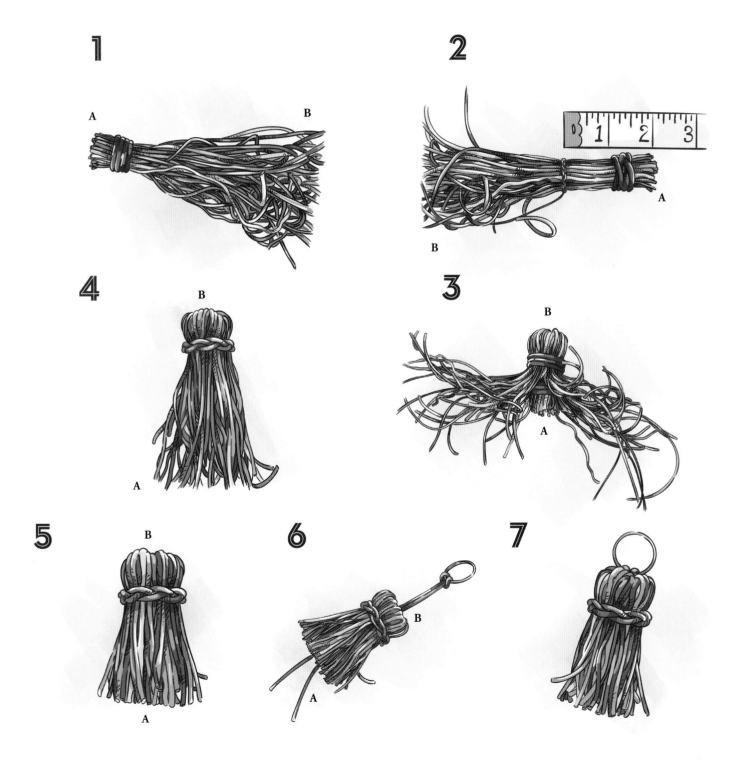

DESERT MOON LEATHER COIL EARRINGS

THIS EARRING PROJECT IS VERY EASY TO MAKE AND IS IDEAL FOR LEATHER-BRAIDING BEGINNERS. EACH EARRING IS MADE USING ONE 1.5-MM LEATHER CORD AND TWO WOODEN BEADS WITH 3-MM OPENINGS.

TOOLS

Measuring tape

Scissors

MATERIALS

2 earring hooks

2 x 10-in. (25-cm) lengths of 1.5-mm brown round leather cord

2 x 30-in (76-cm) lengths of 0.5-mm brown round leather cord

2 pairs of matching wooden beads with 3-mm openings

1 For each earring, thread one of the earring hooks onto one of the 1.5-mm brown leather cords. Position the hook at 1½-in. (4-cm).

2 Fold over the end of the leather cord slightly and thread a wooden bead of your choice onto both cords. Here, we have used a cylinder bead.

3 Thread the other style of wooden bead—in this case, a circular bead—onto the longer of the leather cords. Position it 1½-in. (4-cm) from the cylindrical bead.

4 Ensuring that the circular bead does not move, fold over the longer end of leather cord and trim it where it meets the cylindrical bead (i.e., so that the cord is approximately 1½-in./4-cm long).

5 Take one of the 0.5-mm brown leather cords and wrap it tightly around the 1.5-mm leather cords, starting at end A and finishing at end B. Make a Finishing Knot (see *Basic Techniques*, page 23) at end B.

1

2

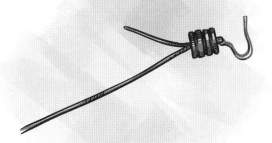

3

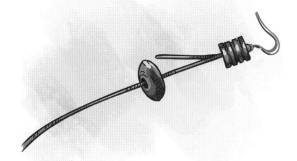

4

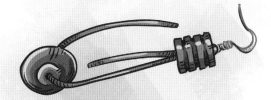

5

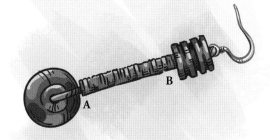

RIVER BREEZE DOUBLE KNOT EARRINGS

THESE EARRINGS ARE MADE WITH TWO PAIRS OF PRETTY CERAMIC BEADS STABILIZED BY A KNOT AT EACH END. ANY TYPE OF CERAMIC BEADS WITH 3-MM OPENINGS CAN BE USED.

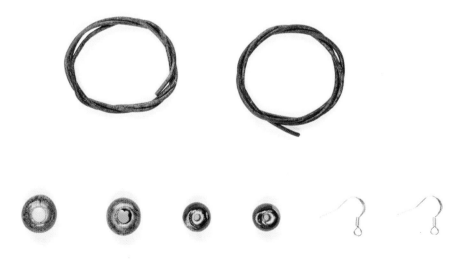

TOOLS

Measuring tape

Scissors

MATERIALS

2 earring hooks

2 x 15-in. (38-cm) lengths of 1.5-mm gray round leather cords

2 pairs of ceramic beads with 3-mm openings

1 For each earring, thread the earring hook onto one of the gray leather cords, so that it is sitting in the middle of the cord.

2 Place end A of the leather cord on top of your index finger and take end B behind your finger. Make a loop with end B in front of your finger, as shown.

3 Take end A of the leather cord and weave it through the loop. Weave it under at point 1, over at point 2, under at point 3, and over at point 4.

4 Take end B of the leather cord and move it counterclockwise, looping it under at point 1 and then through the center at point 2.

5 Take end A of the leather cord and move it counterclockwise, looping it under at point 1 and then through the center at point 2.

6 Pull both ends of leather cord toward the earring hook.

7 Thread two different ceramic beads onto both ends of the leather cord and repeat Steps 2–6.

8 You have now completed the second knot.

9 To finish, trim off the excess cords at this second knot.

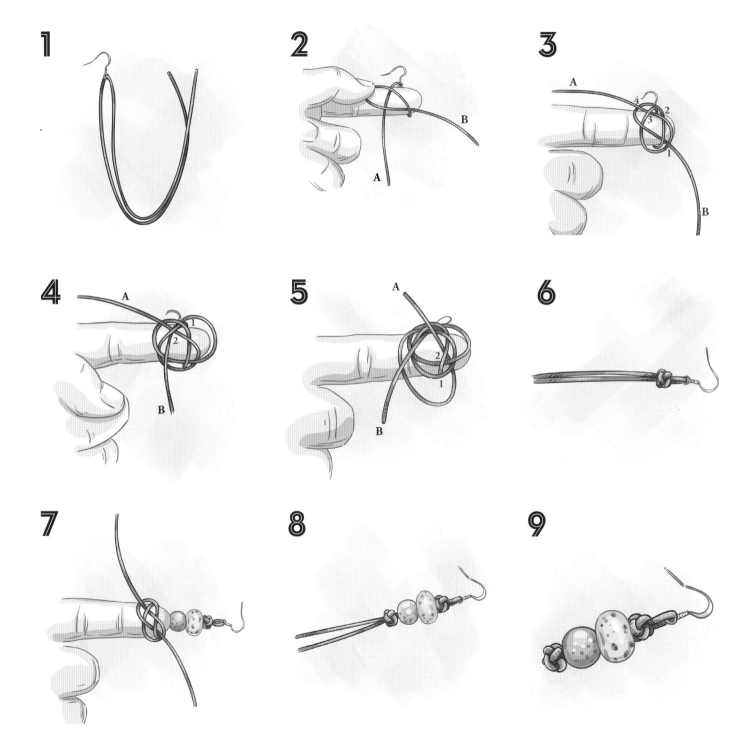

RED LANTERN EARRINGS

THIS PAIR OF EARRINGS USES A BASIC WEAVING TECHNIQUE TO MAKE THE CIRCULAR PATTERN, BUT THE FINISHED DESIGN IS VERY DIFFERENT.

TOOLS

Measuring tape

Scissors

Ring sizer

MATERIALS

2 earring hooks

2 x 25-in. (64-cm) lengths of 2-mm natural red round leather cords

1 For each earring, take one of the red leather cords and wrap it around the ring sizer at the size 3 mark. In this project, end A is the fixed end and end B is the braiding end. To start, place end B on top of end A, as shown.

2 Take end B and wrap it around the stick once, passing under at point 1, through point 2, and over at point 3.

3 Turn the ring sizer over, so that end A is on the right-hand side and end B is on the left-hand side. Move end B over end A, so that they overlap at points 1 and 2.

4 Place end B through and under the opening at point 1 and then through and under the opening at point 2.

5 Turn the ring sizer over. End A and end B should be in their original positions. Take end B through the opening at end A to finish the circular braid.

6 Slide the woven piece off the ring sizer. The area around end A (at the top of the ball) will be where you attach the earring hook. End B, therefore, is at the bottom. Take end B and carefully follow the path of the A cord, weaving it in a circular motion three times.

7 When end B arrives at the bottom end for the last time, you will see five complete sets of weaves, one set with two strands and four sets with three strands. Take end B and loop it through the opening in the center of the ball so that it comes out at the top by end A.

8 Loop end B through the opening in the earring hook. Trim off end A or hide it in the belly of the ball. Take end B and loop it back through the center opening from the top to the bottom end.

9 The earring hook should now be securely looped in by end B, which is now positioned at the bottom end of the ball. Take end B and finish weaving to complete the round structure. The finished ball should have five sets of three strands from any observation point. Trim off any excess cords and press lightly with your fingers to shape the ball until it is round and even.

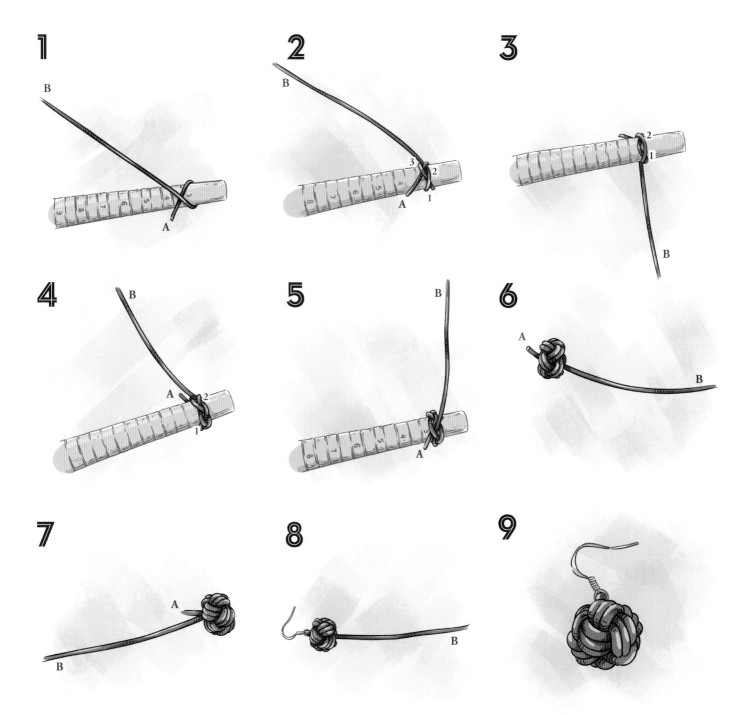

BELT BUCKLE

USING THE TECHNIQUES DEMONSTRATED IN THIS PROJECT, YOU WILL BE ABLE TO TRANSFORM AN EVERYDAY ITEM INTO SOMETHING SPECIAL BY UPGRADING A VINTAGE METAL BELT BUCKLE.

TOOLS

Measuring tape

Scissors

Glue

MATERIALS

Vintage metal belt buckle

A length of 1-mm natural brown round leather cord

1 Wrap the leather cord once around the belt buckle. The fixed end for this project is end A and the expanding end is end B. Overlap the two ends at point 1, as shown.

2 Wrap end B around the belt buckle one more time, to form a second point of overlap at point 2.

3 Weave end B of the leather cord under the overlap at point 1 and the overlap at point 2. Tighten the leather cord.

4 Wrap end B of the leather cord once around the buckle, forming another overlap at point 3. Weave end B under the overlap you made prior to the overlap at point 3. This is the repeating step.

5 Keep repeating Step 4 until the first side of the belt buckle is covered with leather cord. Stabilize the braid using a Spanish Ring Knot (see *Basic Techniques*, page 20).

6 Repeat Steps 1–5 to cover the other side of the belt buckle with braided leather cord.

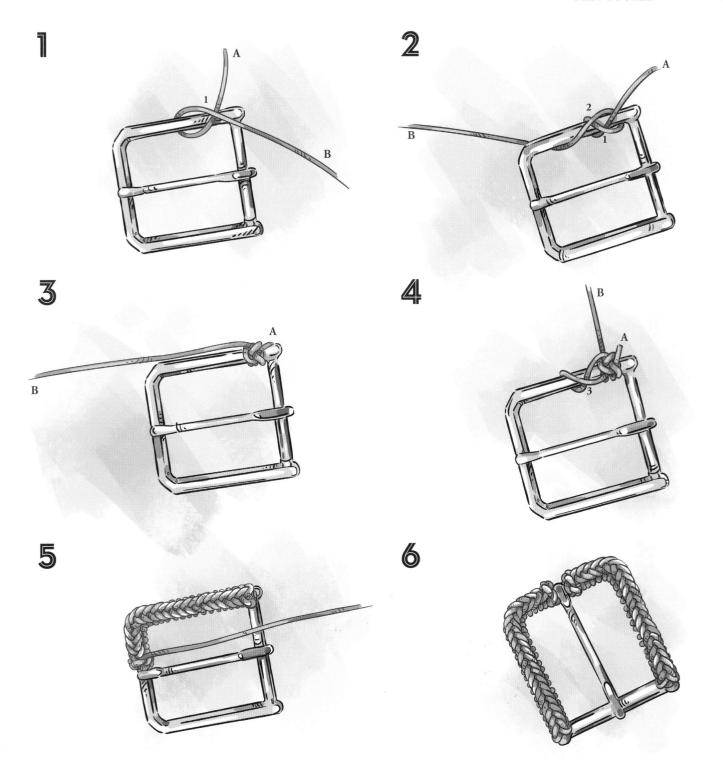

WRAPPED HANDLE

THIS IS AN EXCELLENT EXAMPLE OF HOW YOU CAN USE BRAIDING TECHNIQUES TO DECORATE ITEMS IN YOUR HOME.

TOOLS

Measuring tape

Scissors

Round wooden stick with a diameter larger than 1³/₈ in. (3.5 cm)

MATERIALS

Wooden drawer handle with a diameter no larger than 1³/₈ in. (3.5 cm)

1 x 80-in. (203-cm) length of 2-mm natural blue round leather cord

1 Wrap the leather cord once around the wooden stick and overlap it, as shown. Here, the starting end is end A and the expanding end is end B. Divide the circumference of the stick into four equal parts. The first part, where the two ends of the cord overlap, is area 1. From here, moving in a clockwise direction around the stick, designate the other parts areas 2, 3, and 4.

2 Wrap end B around the wooden stick for a second time and form an overlap in area 3 and then under the red dot marked in area 1.

3 Wrap end B around the wooden stick a third time, weaving it under the red dot marked in area 3 and then under the red dot marked in area 2.

4 Wrap end B around the wooden stick for a fourth time, weaving it under the red dot marked in area 4 and then under the two red dots marked in area 2.

5 Take end B around the wooden stick for a fifth time, weaving it under the red dots marked between areas 4 and 1, then under the two red dots marked between areas 2 and 3.

6 Wrap end B around the wooden stick for a sixth time, weaving it under the red dots marked between areas 1 and 2, then under the red dots marked between areas 3 and 4.

7 Remove the finished knot ring from the wooden stick.

8 Wrap the knot ring loosely around the wooden drawer handle.

9 Adjust the cords of the knot ring until you are happy with the effect and then tighten the cords so that the ring fits securely over the handle. Take end B and weave it toward end A one more time. Trim off the excess cords.

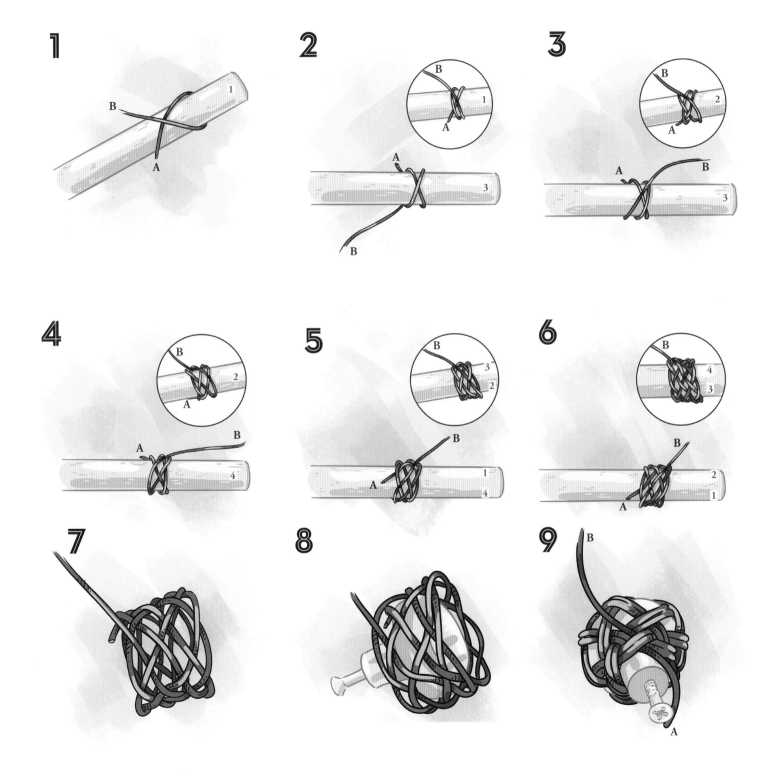

CHAPTER 3

BRAID REFERENCE LIBRARY

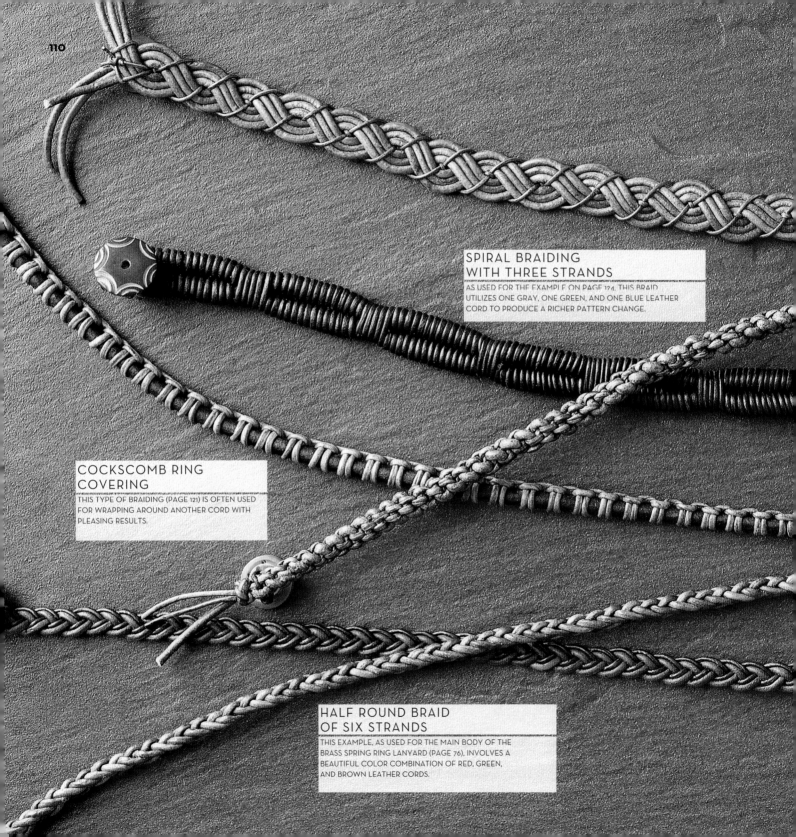

SPIRAL BRAIDING
WITH THREE STRANDS

AS USED FOR THE EXAMPLE ON PAGE 124, THIS BRAID
UTILIZES ONE GRAY, ONE GREEN, AND ONE BLUE LEATHER
CORD TO PRODUCE A RICHER PATTERN CHANGE.

COCKSCOMB RING
COVERING

THIS TYPE OF BRAIDING (PAGE 121) IS OFTEN USED
FOR WRAPPING AROUND ANOTHER CORD WITH
PLEASING RESULTS.

HALF ROUND BRAID
OF SIX STRANDS

THIS EXAMPLE, AS USED FOR THE MAIN BODY OF THE
BRASS SPRING RING LANYARD (PAGE 76), INVOLVES A
BEAUTIFUL COLOR COMBINATION OF RED, GREEN,
AND BROWN LEATHER CORDS.

FLAT BRAIDING OF EIGHT CORDS

AS USED FOR THE EIGHT-STRING NECKWEAR (PAGE 64):
IN THIS EXAMPLE, HOWEVER, THE TWO THINNER CORDS
EMPHASIZE THE ARC-SHAPED LINES OF THE DESIGN.

INFINITY LOOP BRAIDING

HERE, THE INFINITY LOOP PATTERN USED FOR THE
INK-GREEN BRAID WRIST WEAR (PAGE 48) IS BROKEN UP BY
BANDS OF SIMPLE WRAPPING.

SIX STRANDS OF FLAT BRAIDING

THIS BRAID USES SIX INDIVIDUAL CORDS
INSTEAD OF THREE FOLDED IN HALF TO
MAKE SIX WORKING STRANDS, AS FOR
THE FISH KEY RING (PAGE 80).

CROCODILE RIDGE BRAID

THIS BRAIDING USES EIGHT LEATHER CORDS IN THE SAME WAY AS THE CROCODILE RIDGE BRAID (PAGE 123). IN THIS EXAMPLE, HOWEVER, THE CORDS ARE THINNER TO CREATE A FINER BRAID.

SIMPLE BRAID

THIS BRAID USES A SIMILAR TECHNIQUE TO THE WESTERN TASSEL WRIST WEAR (PAGE 44). HOWEVER, ONLY THREE INDIVIDUAL CORDS ARE USED TO PRODUCE A SIMPLER AND NEATER BRAID.

SPIRAL BRAIDING WITH FOUR STRANDS

THIS BRAID USES THE SAME TECHNIQUE AS THE FIRST FIVE STEPS OF THE SIX-STRING WRAP NECKLACE (SEE PAGE 72), BUT WITH THINNER CORDS, WHICH PRODUCES A NEATER BRAID THAT WOULD WORK WELL AS A BRACELET.

THREE RINGS COVERING

USED IN THE EXAMPLE ON PAGE 122, THIS BRAID SHOWS
THE STUNNING EFFECT OF CHANGING THE COLOR
OF THE WRAPPING CORD HALFWAY THROUGH.

FLAT BRAIDING WITH
FIVE STRANDS

THIS KIND OF PLAIN WEAVING (SEE PAGE 125) CAN BE
MODIFIED TO CREATE A STRAIGHT LINE OR CURVE.

FLAT BRAIDING

USING A SIMILAR TECHNIQUE TO STEPS 6-7 OF THE WESTERN TASSEL
WRIST WEAR (SEE PAGE 44), THIS PIECE WEAVES THREE SEPARATE
CORDS IN A PRETTY COLORWAY.

BUCKLE COVERING BRAID

AS SEEN IN THE BELT BUCKLE (SEE PAGE 100), THIS BRAID IS
USED TO WRAP A LEATHER CORD, PROVING THAT THIS
TECHNIQUE NEED NOT BE LIMITED TO BELT BUCKLES.

SQUARE STITCH KNOT

THIS BRAID (SEE PAGE 119) USES A COMMON
METHOD FOR MAKING A SERIES OF KNOTS.

SQUARE KNOTS WITH TWO STRANDS

LIKE THE SIX-STRING WRAP NECKLACE (SEE PAGE 72), THIS IS AN EXAMPLE OF HOW THE SQUARE KNOTS WITH TWO STRANDS TECHNIQUE CAN BE USED TO EMBELLISH A PIECE OF SPIRAL BRAIDING.

CROCODILE RIDGE BRAID WITH TWO OUTER HALF-ROUND RIDGES WITH EIGHT STRINGS

THIS TYPE OF BRAIDING (SEE PAGE 123) IS OFTEN USED TO MAKE A BELT, AS IT CREATES A FLAT, WIDE BRAID THAT IS COMFORTABLE TO WEAR.

FLAT BRAIDING WITH FOUR STRANDS

IN THIS VERSION OF THE BRAID ON PAGE 120, THE THINNER BLACK CORDS SERVE TO EMPHASIZE THE CURVES OF THE BRAID.

SIX STRANDS OF FLAT BRAIDING

USING THREE CORDS FOLDED IN HALF TO MAKE SIX WORKING STRANDS, AS FOR THE FISH KEY RING (SEE PAGE 80), THIS PIECE USES CORDS WITH A LARGER DIAMETER TO CREATE A WIDER BRAID.

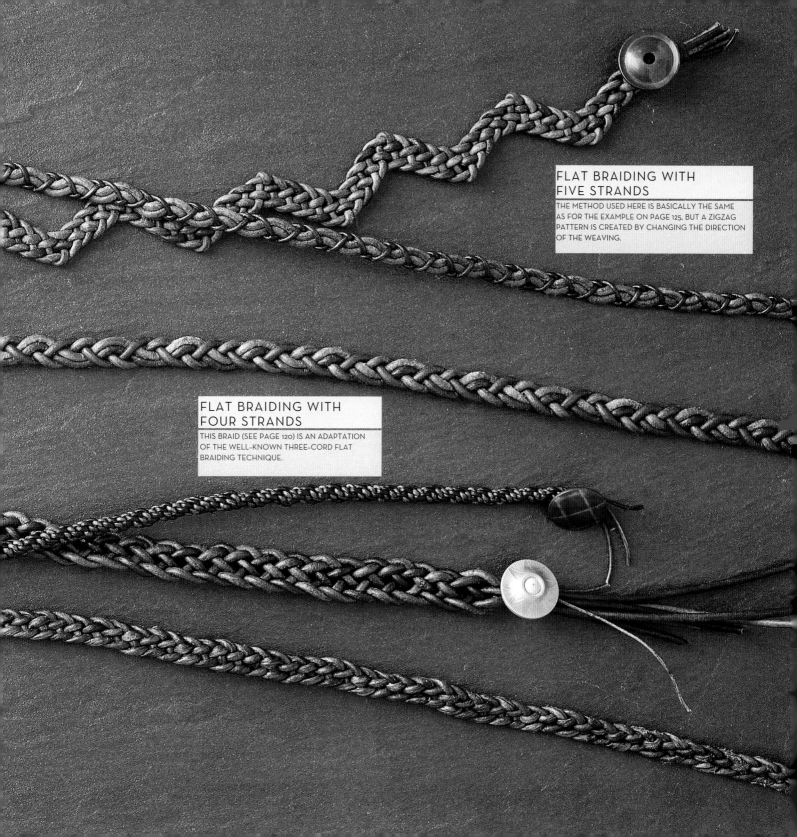

FLAT BRAIDING WITH FIVE STRANDS

THE METHOD USED HERE IS BASICALLY THE SAME AS FOR THE EXAMPLE ON PAGE 125, BUT A ZIGZAG PATTERN IS CREATED BY CHANGING THE DIRECTION OF THE WEAVING.

FLAT BRAIDING WITH FOUR STRANDS

THIS BRAID (SEE PAGE 120) IS AN ADAPTATION OF THE WELL-KNOWN THREE-CORD FLAT BRAIDING TECHNIQUE.

AUSTRALIAN FLAT BRAID

THIS IS A COMMON STARTING BRAID FOR BRAIDING BELTS. IT IS ESPECIALLY GOOD FOR ANY PIECE OF FLAT BRAIDING THAT USES TWO OR MORE CORDS.

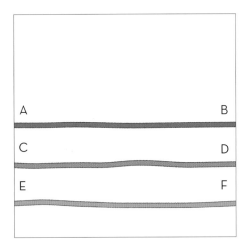

1 Lay out the three leather cords horizontally, as shown. The ends of the purple cord are ends A and B; the ends of the green cord are ends C and D; and the ends of the brown cord are ends E and F.

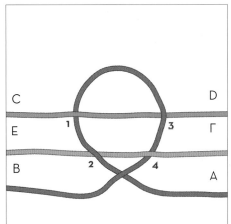

2 Take end A under at point 1 and over at point 2. Take end B over at point 3 and under at point 4. Overlap ends A and B, placing B on top of A.

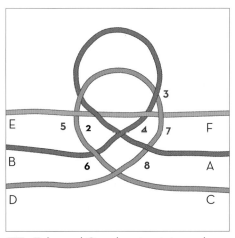

3 Take end C under at point 5 and over at point 6. Take end D over at point 7 and under at point 8. Overlap ends C and D, placing D on top of C.

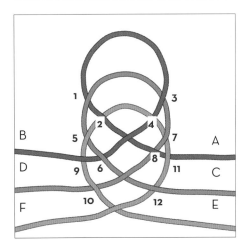

4 Take end E under at point 9 and over at point 10. Take end F over at point 11 and under at point 12. Overlap ends E and F, placing F on top of E. This completes the first cycle of braiding.

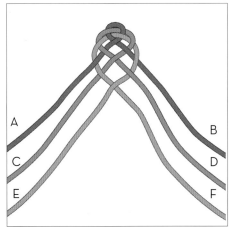

5 Tighten the three cords to stabilize them, then separate them out so that you have six cords to work with once more. Label the cords as per Step 1, so that end A of the purple cord is on the left and end B is on the right, and so on. Repeat Steps 2–5 until you reach the desired length of braiding.

SQUARE STITCH KNOT

THIS IS A COMMON METHOD FOR MAKING A SERIES OF KNOTS AND CAN BE USED TO CREATE LENGTHS OF BOTH FLAT AND ROUND BRAIDING.

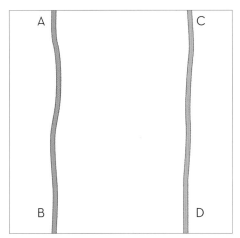

1 Lay out the two leather cords vertically, as shown. The ends of the green cord are ends A and B and the ends of the brown cord are ends C and D.

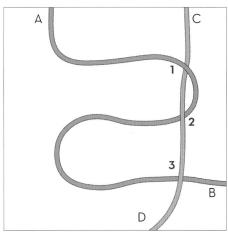

2 Take end B over at point 1, under at point 2, and under at point 3.

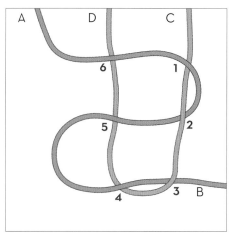

3 Take end D under at points 4, 5, and 6.

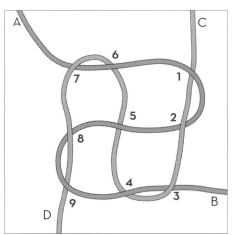

4 Take end D over at points 7 and 8, and then under at point 9.

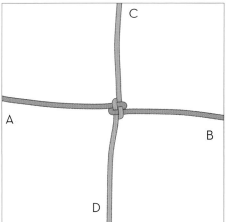

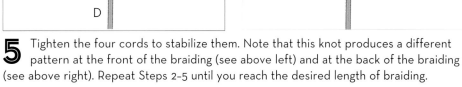

5 Tighten the four cords to stabilize them. Note that this knot produces a different pattern at the front of the braiding (see above left) and at the back of the braiding (see above right). Repeat Steps 2–5 until you reach the desired length of braiding.

FLAT BRAIDING WITH FOUR STRANDS

THIS IS A FORM OF FLAT BRAIDING USING FOUR CORDS, WHICH IS SIMPLY AN ADAPTATION OF THE WELL-KNOWN THREE-CORD FLAT BRAIDING TECHNIQUE.

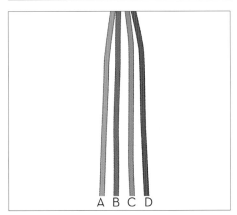

1 Lay out the four leather cords vertically, as shown. The brown cord is A, the purple cord is B, the green cord is C, and the red cord is D.

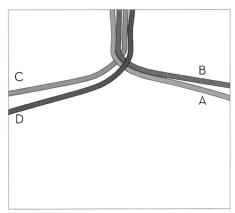

2 Take cords A and B over cord C and under cord D.

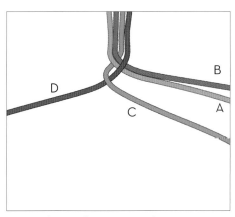

3 Take cord C over cord D.

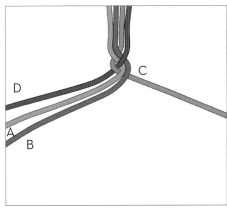

4 Take cords A and B over cord C.

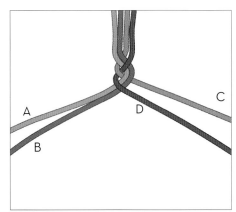

5 Take cord D over cords A and B.

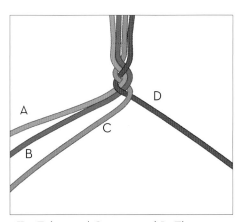

6 Take cord C over cord D. This completes the first cycle of braiding. The four colored cords should now be in the same position as they were in Step 1. Repeat Steps 2–6 until you reach the desired length of braiding.

COCKSCOMB RING COVERING

THIS TYPE OF BRAIDING IS OFTEN USED FOR WRAPPING AROUND ANOTHER CORD.

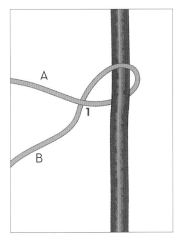 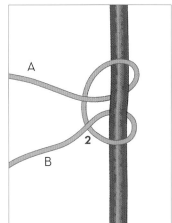 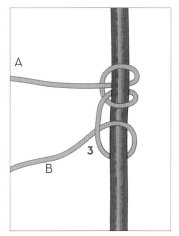 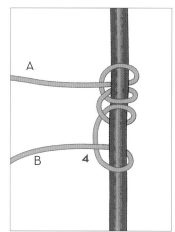

1 For this technique, the starting end of the thinner light brown cord is end A and the expanding end is end B. Take end B of the light brown cord and wrap it counterclockwise under and then over the dark brown cord, ensuring that end A overlaps end B at point 1 (as shown).

2 Take end B and wrap it counterclockwise once more, but this time bring it over and then under the dark brown cord, ensuring that it overlaps itself at point 2. This is the start of the braid.

3 Pull the light brown cord tight, then take end B and wrap it counterclockwise under and then over the dark brown cord again, but this time make sure that it goes under itself at point 3.

4 Tighten the light brown cord, sliding the new loop up the dark brown cord to sit neatly with the first loops. Take end B and wrap it counterclockwise over and then under the dark brown cord, forming an overlap at point 4. Repeat Steps 2–4 until you have covered the desired length of braiding.

THREE RINGS COVERING

THIS IS A FOUR-STRING BRAID IN WHICH A TRIANGULAR SHAPE IS FORMED BY WRAPPING ONE CORD AROUND THREE OTHER CORDS.

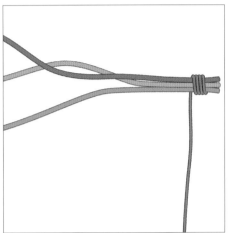

1 Gather together the ends of the brown, green, and purple leather cords to form a triangle and bind the ends with the length of red leather cord.

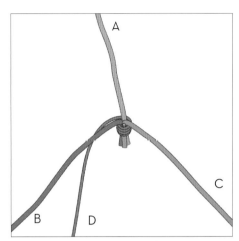

2 Sit the three main cords on their bound ends and splay them out. Label the brown cord A, the purple cord B, the green cord C, and the red cord D.

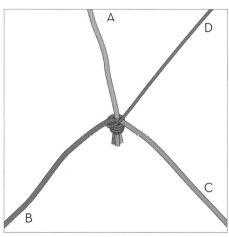

3 Take cord D and bring it under cord B, then place it between cords A and C.

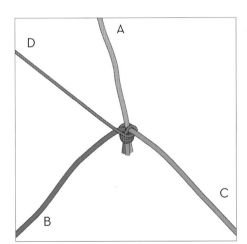

4 Take cord D again, but this time bring it under cord C and place it between cords A and B.

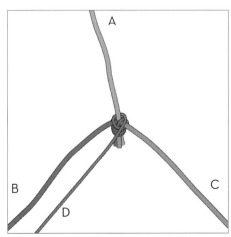

5 Take cord D once more and bring it under cord A and over cord C, then place it between cords B and C.

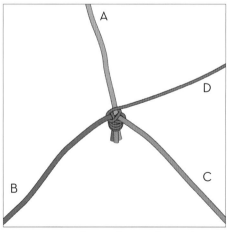

6 Bring cord D under cord B and over cord A, placing it between cords A and C. This completes one cycle. Repeat Steps 4–6 until you reach the desired length of braiding.

CROCODILE RIDGE BRAID WITH TWO OUTER HALF-ROUND RIDGES WITH EIGHT STRINGS

THIS TYPE OF BRAIDING IS OFTEN USED FOR A BRAIDED BELT, BECAUSE IT CREATES A FLAT, WIDE BRAID THAT IS COMFORTABLE TO WEAR.

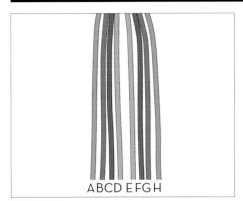

1 Arrange the eight leather cords vertically, as shown. Label the cords A to H, from left to right.

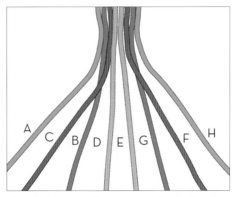

2 Take cord C over cord B, placing it between cords A and B. Take cord F over cord G, placing it between cords G and H.

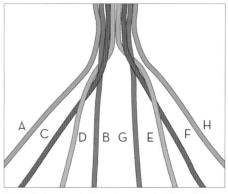

3 Take cord D under cords C and B, placing it between cords C and B. Take cord E under cords F and G, placing it between cords G and F.

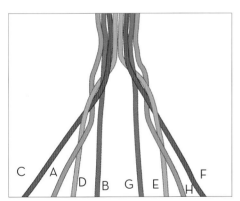

4 Take cord A under cords C and D, then place it between cords C and D. Take cord H under cords E and F, then place it between cords E and F. Relabel the cords A to H, from left to right.

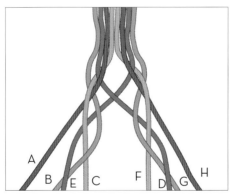

5 Take cord D over cord E and under cords F and G, then place it between cords F and G. Take cord E under cords B and C, then place it between cords B and C.

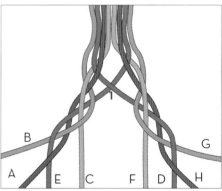

6 Take cord A under cords B and E, then place it between cords B and E. Take cord H under cords D and G, then place it between cords D and G. Cords D and E should cross over at point 1. Repeat Steps 5–6, relabeling the cords A to H, from left to right, before you repeat these steps each time, until you reach the desired length of braiding.

SPIRAL BRAIDING WITH THREE STRANDS

THIS TECHNIQUE PRODUCES A SIMPLE, BUT THREE-DIMENSIONAL, PIECE OF BRAIDING. THE VARIATIONS BASED ON THIS BRAID CAN YIELD SURPRISINGLY DIFFERENT PATTERNS AND END RESULTS WHEN DIFFERENT THICKNESSES AND COLORS OF LEATHER CORD ARE USED.

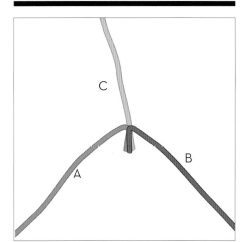

1 Gather together the ends of the three leather cords to form a triangle. Sit the cords on their bound ends and splay them out. Label them A, B, and C, moving counterclockwise.

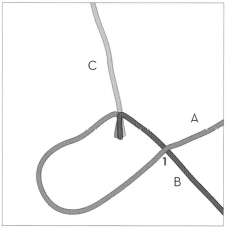

2 Take cord A over cord B, forming an overlap at point 1.

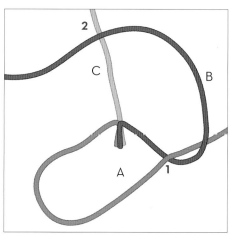

3 Take cord B over cord A, then bring it up and counterclockwise to sit over cord C, forming another overlap at point 2.

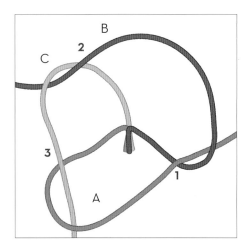

4 Take cord C over cord B and down through the opening formed by cord A, forming a final overlap at point 3.

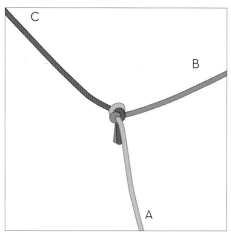

5 Tighten cords A, B, and C. This completes the first cycle of braiding. Relabel the cords B, C, and A, moving counterclockwise. Repeat Steps 2–5 until you reach the desired length of braiding.

FLAT BRAIDING WITH FIVE STRANDS

THIS KIND OF PLAIN WEAVING CAN BE MODIFIED IN MANY WAYS. YOU CAN MAKE THE BRAIDING IN A STRAIGHT LINE OR A CURVE, AND THE BENDING CAN EVEN BE MADE NEARLY AT A RIGHT ANGLE.

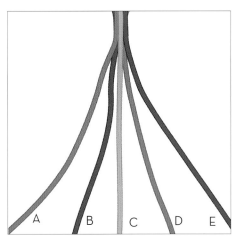

1 Gather together the ends of the five blue leather cords and line them up, labeling them A, B, C, D, and E, from left to right.

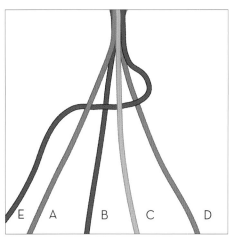

2 Bring cord E over to the left, passing it over cord D, under cord C, over cord B, and under cord A.

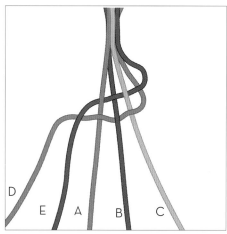

3 Bring cord D over to the left, passing it over cord C, under cord B, over cord A, and under cord E.

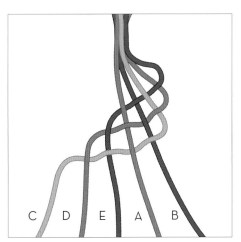

4 Bring cord C over to the left, passing it over cord B, under cord A, over cord E, and under cord D.

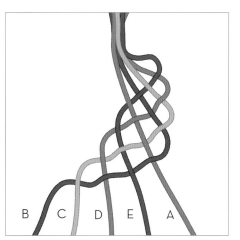

5 Bring cord B over to the left, passing it over cord A, under cord E, over cord D, and under cord C.

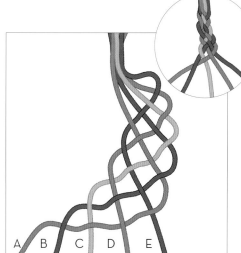

6 Bring cord A over to the left, passing it over cord E, under cord D, over cord C, and under cord B. Tighten the cords. This repeats one sequence of braiding. Repeat Steps 2–6 until you reach the desired length of braiding.

INDEX

CREDITS

WE WOULD LIKE TO DEDICATE THIS BOOK TO OUR LOVED ONES, TO COMMEMORATE THE TIMES WE HAVE SHARED WORKING ON THIS BOOK TOGETHER.

Quarto would like to give a special thanks to Leather Cord USA for supplying some of the leather cords for photography.

WWW.LEATHERCORDUSA.COM